Students with Disabilities, Learning Difficulties and Disadvantages in the Baltic States, South Eastern Europe and Malta

EDUCATIONAL POLICIES AND INDICATORS

ORGANISATION FOR ECONOMIC CO-OPERATION AND DEVELOPMENT

The OECD is a unique forum where the governments of 30 democracies work together to address the economic, social and environmental challenges of globalisation. The OECD is also at the forefront of efforts to understand and to help governments respond to new developments and concerns, such as corporate governance, the information economy and the challenges of an ageing population. The Organisation provides a setting where governments can compare policy experiences, seek answers to common problems, identify good practice and work to co-ordinate domestic and international policies.

The OECD member countries are: Australia, Austria, Belgium, Canada, the Czech Republic, Denmark, Finland, France, Germany, Greece, Hungary, Iceland, Ireland, Italy, Japan, Korea, Luxembourg, Mexico, the Netherlands, New Zealand, Norway, Poland, Portugal, the Slovak Republic, Spain, Sweden, Switzerland, Turkey, the United Kingdom and the United States. The Commission of the European Communities takes part in the work of the OECD.

OECD Publishing disseminates widely the results of the Organisation's statistics gathering and research on economic, social and environmental issues, as well as the conventions, guidelines and standards agreed by its members.

JOINT RESEARCH CENTRE (European Commision)

The mission of the Joint Research Centre is to provide customer-driven scientific and technical support for the conception, development, implementation and monitoring of European Union policies. As a service of the European Commission, the Joint Research Centre functions as a reference centre of science and technology for the Union. Close to the policy-making process, it serves the common interest of the Member States, while being independent of special interests, whether private or national.

This work is published on the responsibility of the Secretary-General of the OECD. The opinions expressed and arguments employed herein do not necessarily reflect the official views of the Organisation for Economic Co-operation and Development or of the governments of its member countries or those of the European Commission - Joint Research Centre (JRC).

ISBN 978-92-64-07582-5 (print)
ISBN 978-92-64-07686-0 (PDF)

Corrigenda to OECD publications may be found on line at: *www.oecd.org/publishing/corrigenda*.

Foreword

In 2007, the Centre for Research on Lifelong Learning (CRELL) and the Directorate General for Education and Culture of the European Commission initiated a joint research study with the Education Directorate of the OECD on Indicators on the Educational Provision for Students with Disabilities, learning Difficulties and Disadvantages. This volume is the output of the collaboration and builds on previous OECD work in this field. In 1995, the OECD's Centre for Educational Research and Innovation (CERI) published the first set of comparable data in the field of special needs education. This work strengthened the view that a different comparative framework would need to be developed if reliable and valid comparisons were to be made. In 1996 the first discussions began with country representatives on developing a resource-based definition to overcome different national interpretations of concepts such as special educational needs which cover very different populations of students experiencing difficulties in accessing the curriculum.

At the same time the UNESCO standards for classifying education systems (ISCED) were in the process of being revised and the definition of special needs education was updated and reformulated to reflect policy developments. In doing so, a much wider range of students, in all types of schools, were brought into the frame. In addition, the idea that extra resourcing may be needed to support schools in helping students access the curriculum more effectively was included in the new description.

It became clear, early on, that for policy relevant comparisons to emerge, a resource-based approach would require that the students included under this definition would need to be subdivided into some form of straightforward classification scheme. Countries agreed on a tri-partite system with three cross-national categories, A, B and C. Briefly, these cover:

- Students with disabilities or impairments viewed in medical terms as organic disorders attributable to organic pathologies (*e.g.* in relation to sensory, motor or neurological defects). The educational need is considered to arise primarily from problems attributable to these disabilities (cross-national category "A/Disabilities").

- Students with behavioural or emotional disorders, or specific difficulties in learning. The educational need is considered to arise primarily from problems in the interaction between the student and the educational context (cross-national category "B/Difficulties").

- Students with disadvantages arising primarily from socio-economic, cultural, and/or linguistic factors. The educational need is to compensate for the disadvantages attributable to these factors (cross-national category "C/Disadvantages").

The data provided in this book are based on the application of this model to Bosnia and Herzegovina, Bulgaria, Croatia, Estonia, Kosovo, Latvia, Lithuania, Malta, Montenegro, Serbia and Slovenia.

This volume presents a full account of the development of the work, and provides qualitative data to contextualise the quantitative information. It provides breakdowns by national category systems as well as comparisons using the cross-national framework described.

The book also follows on earlier work carried out by OECD on economies in South Eastern Europe on children at risk and those with disabilities and expands it to include the Baltic States and Malta. It describes the continuation of a process intended to improve the quality of policy analysis through the development of internationally comparable data.

The work was supported in 2007-2009 by contributions from OECD (*e.g.* World Bank, Belgium) as well as from Directorate General Education and Culture (Unit A4) and the Centre for Research on Lifelong Learning (CRELL), Directorate General Joint Research Centre, European Commission; in-kind additional funds were provided from the following participating countries: Finland, Germany, Estonia and Croatia.

The book was prepared by Peter Evans of the OECD Secretariat and Marcella Deluca of CRELL, DG Joint Research Centre, European Commission. The statistical work was carried out by Philippe Hervé of the OECD Secretariat. The synthesis country report in Chapter 6 was produced by Lani Florian, Martyn Rouse and Majda Becirevic of Aberdeen University in collaboration with Peter Evans and Gerhard Kowar of the OECD Secretariat and Marcella Deluca of CRELL. The work reported on PISA in Chapter 7 of the book was carried out by Barbara LeRoy, Preethy Samuel, and Peter Bahr of Wayne State University with Peter Evans and Marcella Deluca. Overall co-ordination and substantive support was provided by the Programme for Co-operation with Non-member Economies of the OECD Directorate for Education.

The countries and economies involved in the study collaborated closely in all the stages of the work reported in this monograph.

Table of contents

Executive Summary

Introduction

Concerns about equity in education, the declining numbers of children and increased demands of the labour market are forcing education systems to take more interest in the educational progress of students who would otherwise under-achieve by offering considerable extra resources to help them learn more effectively. Providing equitable systems of education to promote the development of all children is an important goal for governments.

Through the ratification of the UN Convention on the Rights of the Child (1989) countries committed themselves to an equitable system of education, and with the signing of the UN Convention on the Rights of Persons with Disabilities (2007) countries fully recognise the right of people with disabilities to education. This is reiterated in the plan of 'Education for All' which requires full educational rights for all children by 2015, *i.e.* a full course of free, compulsory primary schooling for all boys and girls, thus including students with disabilities, learning difficulties and disadvantages.

For the European Union (EU), the domain of Special Education Needs is part of the wider agenda promoted by the Lisbon Strategy and has been emphasised with the Coherent Framework on Indicators and Benchmarks, the Council Conclusions of May 2007, and the Council Conclusions of May 2009 on a Strategic Framework for European Cooperation in Education and Training. Special education needs is an area that requires more information in order to promote and monitor inclusive policies *vis-à-vis* the education of students with disabilities, learning difficulties and disadvantages.

Developing an internationally comparable framework: the resource-based definition

Over the past thirty years, an increasing number of countries have established educational policies that target extra money and resources to students who, for various reasons, are unable to access school curricula as easily as some of their peers. Students receiving these extra resources have come to be formally categorised by the international community as having disabilities, learning difficulties, and disadvantages. These three descriptors are purposefully broad and intended to capture various types of students, from those who confront physical and cognitive disabilities to those who are socio-economically disadvantaged.

This framework was promoted by OECD and it has distinctive features: 1) it is compatible with a social model of disability; 2) it is based on the ISCED 97 (International Standard Classification of Education) definition of special needs education; and 3) it introduces the important notion that extra resources are needed to assist schools in helping students with a broad range of learning challenges (often referred to as those with special educational needs [SEN]) to access the curriculum more effectively. Such a resource-based approach brings together a heterogeneous group of students which is further subdivided into a tripartite taxonomy based on perceived causes of educational failure covering: A Disabilities, B Difficulties, and C Disadvantages. This classification is innovative because it allows for internationally valid comparisons that help to overcome the different meanings of special education needs in different countries.

The joint research study

Research conducted since January 2007 by the OECD, the European Commission (CRELL and Directorate General for Education and Culture), and a cadre of independent researchers has allowed for an augmentation of the data quantity and quality of the OECD's SENDDD database by expanding the work on statistics and indicators for students with disabilities, learning difficulties and disadvantages in new countries in order to: 1) improve and incorporate educational data and other qualitative information on special needs students into the international comparative framework used by other EU/OECD countries; 2) develop comparative indicators covering issues relevant to the education of these students; 3) strengthen the quantity, quality, reliability and comparability of qualitative and quantitative data on students with special educational needs.

The data collected are based on the application of this model to the following EU and accession countries: Bulgaria, Croatia, Estonia, Latvia, Lithuania, Malta, Slovenia, and Romania as well as non-member economies: Bosnia and Herzegovina, Kosovo, Moldova, Montenegro, and Serbia. This volume presents quantitative and qualitative data for school year 2005-2006.

Main findings

This book provides an internationally comparable set of indicators on the educational provision for students with disabilities, learning difficulties and disadvantages (SENDDD). It highlights the number of students concerned, where they are educated - special schools, special classes and regular classes and in what phases of education – pre-primary, compulsory and upper secondary education. It also discusses policy implications *vis-à-vis* special education needs.

This monograph is divided into two parts. In the first part, chapters one to five provide qualitative and quantitative data on students with disabilities, learning difficulties and disadvantages based on the completion of the electronic questionnaire used by OECD to gather data in the SENDDD project. In the second part, chapter six provides a more detailed account of the process through which these data are developed and gathered. Chapter seven gives an account of data gathered on SEN students in SEE countries and Baltic States involved in PISA 2006. Chapter eight discusses the results and draws out policy implications.

National systems of education have developed procedures and practices for defining, identifying and resourcing students who have difficulties in accessing the curriculum. This is determined mainly by reference to national concepts and understanding based in cultural history and law making. International comparisons provide contrasts against which these assumptions can be re-analysed and re-conceptualised. The work carried out has shown that:

- The *classification* of students with disabilities, learning difficulties and disadvantages varies among participating economies; some use 3 categories while others use 10.

- The numbers of students included vary widely, within comparable categories of disability. For instance, some countries identify and provide additional educational resources for ten times as many blind and partially sighted students as other countries.

- The *place* of education also varies substantially with some countries educating all students with disabilities in regular schools while others educate almost all of them in special schools. In some countries, children from socio-economically disadvantaged backgrounds are educated in segregated settings in contradistinction to most EU and OECD countries. Equity considerations lead to the position that students with disadvantages be educated in regular, mainstream schools rather than in separate institutions. The educational and social experiences of special schools and regular schools are different, and this could be inequitable in terms of students' access to post-compulsory education and the labour market.

- Further research on the *place* of education shows substantial variation both in the proportions of students identified as well as in the place of education. For Category A the proportions identified are close to the OECD averages. However, for Category B there are substantial differences with fewer students being supported especially in upper secondary education. This is an unsatisfactory outcome and the reasons need to be identified and rectified. More investment may well be necessary at least in the short to medium terms to support these students more effectively and to provide teachers and schools with the necessary skills to help to keep them in school. More access to vocational training, which is substantially less for these countries and economies than for other EU and OECD shown by the PISA results, may form part of the solution.

- The *gender* differences are marked with the ratio of boys to girls identified for different programmes and given additional resources being in the order of 3 to 2. This study shows consistent findings concerning the preponderance of numbers of boys over girls in a wide range of analyses. There are typically more male students receiving additional resources than females, regardless of whether data are analysed by educational setting, cross-national or national category, age of student, or phase of education. These differences should become a priority when countries examine the basis by which students are identified for different programmes, and examine the long-term consequences of participation in those programmes when they are provided in segregated facilities. As in OECD member countries, with the exception of Lithuania, many more boys than girls are provided with additional resources to help them access the curriculum. It is unclear why. If boys genuinely need more help because education systems provide them with inherently more challenges then providing them with more resources is equitable. On the other hand, if the provision made available, *e.g.* special schools or special classes, merely serves to lead to a greater likelihood of social exclusion then it is not equitable. The conclusion would be that these resources should be put into renewing regular education to prevent the systematic exclusion of many students from it as they get older as the data presented in this report reveals.

All of these factors raise questions about the educational practices of any one particular country and have policy implications, especially concerning the efficient and equitable use of funds. Thus the comparative context provides real added value by challenging national assumptions through evidence and data and in the context of global agreements. Furthermore, the appropriate education of students with disabilities, learning difficulties and disadvantages is a key factor in creating social cohesion and inclusion through the efficient use of education provision.

The book also presents an analysis of the participation and performance of students with special education needs in the 2006 implementation of the Programme for International Student Assessment (PISA). A summary of PISA 2006 data is provided as they apply to SEN students in the economies that took part in PISA 2006 namely: Croatia, Estonia, Latvia, Lithuania, Serbia and Slovenia. This report describes the participation rates by countries and the demographic characteristics of the students with special educational needs as a group, as well as by their disability status. Students' educational experiences and perceptions are presented as well as their perceptions of their learning behaviours. In general not enough SEN students are included in PISA from not enough economies and the conclusions that can be drawn are therefore extremely limited.

In comparison to their peers in other parts of the world, the SEN students from the Baltic and the SEE regions all attended public schools and had larger class sizes. While vocational training opportunities were limited across the world, students in these regions had practically no such opportunities. In terms of academic performance, these students performed less well than their peers, with the exception of students with limited test language proficiency, who scored higher than their peers across the world. They also reported the highest use of computers and information technology. Students in the two regions also believed that academic performance was less important than their peers in other parts of the world. Finally, with regard to information technology and computers, students in these two regions have not been using computers as long as in other regions. They use them less in school. However, they use them in the same way as other students across the world and they express more confidence in their ability to use them for high level skills.

Added value

This study offers a unique opportunity for policy makers in the field of special education to be engaged in an on-going construction of new knowledge, based on evidence gathered about the full diversity of students who are having difficulty in accessing the curriculum and thereby failing to benefit fully from education. Including the target economies into this arena has given them the opportunity of learning from others and also influencing the direction of the work. What is innovative about this study is that:

- It brings together policy makers to discuss national practices based on data and indicators.

- It constructs internationally comparative frameworks.

- It provides the opportunity for creating a system of indicators in an area (students with disabilities, difficulties and disadvantages) in which there is currently little data and that will apply across the fore-mentioned economies.

- It agrees on policy relevant indicators that lead to new levels of data collection.

- It supports policy making on inclusive education.

- It contributes to the development of equitable and inclusive education systems.

Conclusion

Providing the correct legal framework for developing inclusive education and the necessary resources and support for SEN students are important elements in developing equitable education systems where all students can benefit as fully as possible from the opportunities education brings. Gathering data is an essential component of developing effective policies and efficient strategies to achieve this goal and to know whether it is being achieved.

All of the data presented in this report indicate the need for reforms in the education systems in these economies in order to improve outcomes for students with special education needs and to create more equitable systems.

More generally, providing opportunities for schools to become learning organisations would allow them to find creative solutions to challenges related to the full diversity of students' abilities. Whether schools are allowed to act in this way is a major policy issue which may require reforms that relinquish some centralised control over the curriculum and school organisation.

Chapter 1. Introduction

Recently an increasing number of countries have established educational policies that allocate extra resources to students who cannot access school curricula as easily as their peers and who have come to be categorised as having disabilities, learning difficulties and disadvantages. Policies geared towards these students demonstrate positive discrimination and operate on the premise that some students require more resources than others in order to achieve equal access to schools and curricula. The goal of this study is then to identify the students and resources involved, develop an internationally comparable framework and link these results to outcome data in order to impact policies in participating economies.

Over the past thirty years, an increasing number of countries have established educational policies that target extra funds and resources for students who, for various reasons, are unable to access school curricula as easily as some of their peers. Students receiving these extra resources have come to be formally categorised by the international community as having disabilities, learning difficulties, and disadvantages (OECD, 2007). These three descriptors are purposefully broad and intended to capture various types of students, from those who confront physical and intellectual disabilities to those who are socio-economically disadvantaged.

Most policies geared toward these three groups of students embrace principles of positive discrimination that attempt to provide equality of educational opportunity for all students. These policies work from the premise that some students will require more resources than others if they are to have equal access to schools and curricula and are based on the 'difference principle' outlined by Rawls (1971). According to Rawls, institutions should be structured with a built-in bias in favour of the disadvantaged because some students require additional help if they are to have the chance to share equally in 'the benefits that education provides opportunities for' (Brighouse, 2000).

Although Rawls' argument originally applied to students with disadvantages, policies of inclusion clearly make it relevant for students with learning difficulties and disabilities (Evans, 2001) and the 'difference principle' is seen in policies of positive discrimination currently in place in various countries. While these policies are diverse in scope and content, they derive not only from a rich literature on best practices for these students, commonly referred to as those with special needs, but have also been recognised and justified in recent years by the international community. Nevertheless, great disparities remain among EU/OECD economies[1] in the allocation of additional resources for students with disabilities, learning difficulties and disadvantages. Thus the ultimate purpose of this work is to identify the students and the resources involved, develop an

---

[1] The term "economies" is used to refer to EU and Accession Member States, OECD member countries and Kosovo.

internationally comparable framework and link these results to outcome data in order to impact policies in EU/OECD member economies (OECD, 2004, 2005 and 2007).

Indeed, as promoted by the EU's Lisbon goals and emphasised within the Coherent Framework on Indicators and Benchmarks and the Council Conclusions of May 2007 (EC, 2007) it is clear that there is a growing international understanding that special educational needs is a topic on which more research and information must be gathered if appropriate policies, such as those aimed at inclusion, are to be promoted and monitored *vis-à-vis* education for students with disabilities, learning difficulties and disadvantages.

The CRELL/OECD study on Indicators on the Educational Provision for Students with Disabilities, learning Difficulties and Disadvantages on from earlier work carried out by OECD on economies in South Eastern Europe (SEE) on children at risk and those with disabilities (OECD, 2006) and expands it to include the Baltic States and Malta. It describes the continuation of a process intended to improve the quality and international comparability of the data available. In this way policy making in the field of education for students with disabilities, learning difficulties and disadvantages will be better informed.

At the beginning of 2007, OECD and the European Commission (EC) strengthened their co-operation in this area with the view:

- In the short to medium term:

  To gather qualitative and quantitative information on students with disabilities, learning difficulties and disadvantages using the OECD conceptual framework - with a view to strengthening the current database on inclusive settings and outcomes, eventually extending the range of indicators to include tertiary education and the development of indicators on inclusive education.

- In the long term:

  To make use of internationally comparable statistics and indicators on students with disabilities, learning difficulties and disadvantages to develop standards and formulate policies for inclusive education which are in line with EU and OECD criteria.

Since the method used to monitor progress within the Lisbon Strategy in the field of education is through the use of indicators and benchmarks, the Centre for the Research on Lifelong Learning (CRELL) based at the Joint Research Centre of the European Commission initiated a research project in this area. The study has been included in CRELL's research domain 'Improving Equity through Education and Training', and aims at addressing the educational provision for students identified as having special educational needs to include those with disabilities, learning difficulties and disadvantages (SENDDD).

The joint study, which involves CRELL, the OECD and DGEAC, also aims to increase the quality and quantity of the data in the OECD's SENDDD database and to expand the OECD work on statistics and indicators by including the EU member and accession economies which are not covered by the OECD study (*i.e.* Malta, Estonia, Latvia, Lithuania, Slovenia, Romania, Bulgaria, and Croatia and FYRoM as well as Bosnia and Herzegovina, Kosovo, Serbia, Montenegro and Moldova) - in order to:

1. Develop procedures for improving and incorporating educational data and other qualitative information on special needs students into the international comparative framework used by other EU/OECD economies.

2. Develop comparative indicators covering issues relevant to the education of students.

3. Strengthen the quantity, quality, reliability and comparability of qualitative and quantitative data on students with special educational needs.

This study also provides the opportunity for creating a system of indicators on SENDDD students that will apply across the above-mentioned economies. For this goal to be achieved, substantial progress will need to be made in strengthening databases in these economies. From the outset the work was planned to become part of the regular OECD data collection using the same methodology across all economies. Project partners were included in all aspects of the work and decisions made on the data gathered, the indicators developed and the content of this publication.

Qualitative and quantitative data were gathered on the education of the students identified above and converted into the international categories of disabilities, learning difficulties and disadvantages. This task was carried out by the member economies involved, the OECD Secretariat and CRELL. CRELL actively supported the research activity and has had access to the full OECD micro datasets. This will allow for a subsequent analysis *vis-à-vis* equity of curriculum access and educational outcomes.

The work was carried out jointly by the Secretariat of the Education Directorate at the OECD and the European Commission (CRELL at the Joint Research Centre and DG Education and Culture) The work was co-ordinated jointly including the organisation of meetings, management group meetings and site visits, as well as the policy reviews and data collection and the publication of the current monograph on indicators. The work reported has benefited from the collaboration with country experts.

The representatives of the target economies were engaged in preparing country reports on special education needs policy as well as in data gathering that was facilitated by the use of an electronic questionnaire developed and maintained by the OECD. Also, economies were invited to participate in meetings of country representatives and were available for site visits.

With the support of CRELL, the EU member and accession economies joined the expert network which supports the work on special education needs at OECD and has become an additional resource for the European Commission on this topic.

Meetings of country representatives and experts

Since the beginning of the joint study, three OECD/CRELL expert meetings have been organised. The first joint OECD/CRELL expert meeting on Indicators on the Educational Provision for Students with Disabilities, learning Difficulties and Disadvantages was held in Helsinki, Finland in May 2007 at the invitation of the Finnish National Board of Education.

The second OECD/CRELL expert meeting took place in Bad Saarow, Germany in October 2007 at the invitation of the Ministry of Education, Science and Research of the

Land of Berlin, the Standing Conference of Ministers of Education, Science and Research and the Federal Ministry of Education and Research. The expert workshops in 2007 were organised back to back with the OECD meetings of country representatives.

The third joint OECD/CRELL expert meeting on Indicators on the Educational Provision for Students with Disabilities, learning Difficulties and Disadvantages was held in Tallinn, Estonia in June 2008 at the invitation of the Ministry of Education and Research.

The final meeting was held in Zagreb, Croatia in April 2009 at the invitation of the National Centre for External Evaluation of Education and the Education and Teacher Training Agency (ETTA).

Information was posted regularly onto the website at the following address: http://crell.jrc.ec.europa.eu/SENDDD

Added value

This study offers a unique opportunity for policy makers in the field of special education to be engaged in an on-going construction of new knowledge, based on evidence gathered about the full diversity of students who are having difficulty in accessing the curriculum and thereby failing to benefit fully from education. Including the target economies into this arena will give them the opportunity of learning from others and also influencing the direction of the work. What is innovative about this study is that:

- It brings together policy makers to discuss national practices based on data and indicators.

- It constructs comparative frameworks.

- It provides the opportunity of creating a system of indicators in an area (students with disabilities, difficulties and disadvantages) where there is currently little data and that will apply across the mentioned economies.

- It agrees on policy relevant indicators that lead to new levels of data gathering.

- It supports policy making on inclusive education.

- It contributes to the development of equitable and inclusive education systems.

Contribution to the UN/EU agenda

The signing of the UN Convention of the Rights of Persons with Disabilities by the EC in 2007 (UN 2006), actions on behalf of the European Parliament, the contents of the Lisbon Strategy of 2000 (EC 2000) all indicate a strong and growing concern that the international community adhere to both the principles and practice of equality of educational opportunity. These international agreements require that special educational needs is fully included in the wider global agenda that has also been pursued by UNESCO through its work on developing Education for All (*e.g.* UNESCO 2006) and via the Millennium Development Goals (www.un.org/millenniumgoals/education.shtml.

The plan of 'Education for All' requires full educational rights for all children by 2015 thus including students with disabilities. Its second objective is to: "Ensure that by 2015 all children, particularly girls, those in difficult circumstances and those belonging to ethnic minorities, have access to and complete, free and compulsory primary education of good quality" (http://portal.unesco.org/education/en).

The target of the UN's Millennium Development Goal No. 2 is to "ensure that, by 2015, children everywhere, boys and girls alike, will be able to complete a full course of primary schooling. Indicators for monitoring progress are: Net enrolment ratio in primary education; Proportion of pupils starting grade 1 who reach last grade of primary; Literacy rate of 15-24 year-olds, women and men"(www.un.org/millenniumgoals/education.shtml)

Providing equitable systems of education to promote the development of all children is an important goal for governments. Through the ratification of the UN Convention on the Rights of the Child (UN 1989) countries committed themselves to an equitable system of education and with the signing of the UN Convention on the Rights of Persons with Disabilities, countries re-emphasised the rights of persons with disabilities to education. "States Parties recognise the right of persons with disabilities to education. With a view to realising this right without discrimination and on the basis of equal opportunity, States Parties shall ensure an inclusive education system at all levels and lifelong learning ….(Art. 24). States Parties undertake to collect appropriate information, including statistical and research data, to enable them to formulate and implement policies to give effect to the present Convention (Art. 31)" (UN, 2006).

The Lisbon Council in 2000 asked European Union governments to take a decisive step to increase social cohesion by 2010. The then heads of state and government agreed upon the three following concrete common objectives: (1) improving the quality and effectiveness of education and training systems in the European Union (EU); (2) facilitating the access of all to education and training systems; and (3) opening up education and training systems to the wider world. The Commission recommends the adoption of the following European benchmarks for EU member states, all effective as of 2010 and based on year 2000 statistics: (1) to halve the rate of early school leavers; (2) to halve the level of gender imbalance among graduates in mathematics, science, and technology and increase the number of graduates; (3) to halve the percentage of low-achieving 15-year-olds in reading, mathematics, and scientific literacy; (4) to ensure that the average percentage of 25-64 year olds with at least upper secondary education will reach 80% or more; and (5) to ensure that the EU-average level of participation in lifelong learning will be at least 15% of the adult working age population and in no country will it be lower than 10% (EC, 2002). Through these actions, they set the objective of "making [European] education and training systems a world quality reference by 2010" (EC, 2000).

The need to ensure that European education and training systems are both efficient and equitable was also reiterated in a decision by the 2006 Spring European Council. As emphasised in the Communication of Efficiency and Equity, investigating equity in education and training implies analysing the extent to which "individuals can take full advantage of education and training, in terms of opportunities, access, treatment and outcomes". Specific issues such as the inclusion of disabled people then need to be monitored. The Communication to the Council and to the European Parliament underlines that education and training policies should combine objectives of efficiency and equity in seeking to maximise their economic and social potential. The domain of Special Education Needs is part of this wider agenda (EC, 2006).

In the draft Council Conclusions on a Coherent Framework of indicators and benchmarks for monitoring progress towards the Lisbon objectives in education and training (ref. 7955/05, adopted by the Council on 25 May 2007) "to make use of, or further develop, sixteen of the proposed core indicators, as outlined below … with regard to those indicators which can largely be based on existing data and whose definition still needs further clarification – special needs education". SEN is then a topic on which more research and information must be gathered if appropriate policies are to be promoted and monitored with regard to students with disabilities, learning difficulties and disadvantages.

Furthermore, the gathering of indicators is strengthened by the Council Conclusions of 24 May 2005 on new indicators in education and training which stress that "full use should be made of existing data and indicators while further efforts should be made to improve their comparability, relevance and timeliness"; Also "there is a need to continue to enhance co-operation with other International Organisations active in this field (*e.g.* OECD, UNESCO, IEA), particularly in order to improve international data coherence". The Council invites the Commission "with regard to indicator areas where international organisations (*e.g.* OECD, UNESCO, and IEA) are planning new surveys, to co-operate with international organisations in order to satisfy the information needs of the EU in indicator areas.

More recent developments include Decision No. 1720/2006/EC of the European Parliament and of the Council of 15 November 2006 which established an action programme in the field of lifelong learning. "In implementing the lifelong programme, due regard shall be paid to ensuring that it contributes fully to furthering the horizontal policies of the Community, in particular by … making provision for learners with special needs, and in particular by helping promote their integration into mainstream education and training.

The Council conclusions of November 2008 on "Preparing young people for the 21st century: an agenda for European co-operation in schools" urge to improve the achievement of learners from migrant or disadvantaged backgrounds, to promote personalised pedagogical approaches and to ensure timely and adequate learning support for all pupils with special needs, whether in mainstream or specialised schools.

In December 2008, the Commission Communication on "An updated strategic framework for European co-operation in education and training" set priority themes for 2009-2010. With regard to learners with special needs: "Promote personalised learning through timely support and well coordinated services. Integrate services within mainstreaming schooling and ensure pathways to further education and training".

Recent Council Conclusions on a Strategic framework for European Co-operation in education and training identified strategic objectives for the period 2010-2020 and underlined the need "to ensure that all learners, including those …with special needs…-complete their education" (Council, May 2009).

Developing an international comparative framework

One of the key elements to achieving an equitable education for all is to develop policies and effective monitoring systems that can provide accountability for the education being offered to all children and can communicate progress in the context of national and international comparisons.

In pursuant of these goals, the OECD has been a source for statistics and indicators on special education needs through the Centre for Educational Research and Innovation (CERI) since the mid 90s. With support, at the outset, from the EC, OECD has developed an international comparative framework based on the definition of special education needs in ISCED 97 (UNESCO, 1997).

ISCED 97 and the resource-based definitions

ISCED 97 provides the following definition of special education: "Special needs education – Educational intervention and support designed to address special educational needs. The term 'special needs education' has come into use as a replacement for the term 'special education'. The older term was mainly understood to refer to the education of children with disabilities that takes place in special schools or institutions distinct from, and outside of, the institutions of the regular school and university system. In many countries today a large proportion of disabled children are in fact educated in institutions of the regular system. Moreover, the concept of 'children with special educational needs' extends beyond those who may be included in handicapped categories to cover those who are failing in school for a wide variety of other reasons that are known to be likely to impede a child's optimal progress. Whether or not this more broadly defined group of children are in need of additional support depends on the extent to which schools need to adapt their curriculum, teaching and organisation and/or to provide additional human or material resources so as to stimulate efficient and effective learning for these pupils".

Applying this definition means that a much wider range of students, in all types of schools, are brought into the framework. In addition, the notion that extra resourcing may be needed to assist schools to help students access the curriculum more effectively is included in the new description. It was accepted that many OECD member countries made additional resources of various kinds available to students who had particular difficulties for a variety of reasons in accessing the regular curriculum whether or not this came within a national definition of special educational needs. This has become the first step in identifying students with disabilities, learning difficulties and disadvantages, *i.e.* those included are those being given additional resources to help them access the curriculum. Thus, the operational definition of special needs education is as follows: **"those with special educational needs are defined by the additional public and/or private resources provided to support their education"**.

Additional resources are those made available over and above the resources generally available to students where no consideration is given to needs of students likely to have particular difficulties in accessing the regular curriculum. Resources can be of many different kinds including personnel resources (*e.g.* additional teachers), material resources (*e.g.* hearing aids, Braille, or modifications to classrooms) and financial resources (*e.g.* favourable funding formulae) (OECD 1998, 2000, 2001, 2003, 2004, 2005 and 2007).

Operational definitions of cross-national categories

However, as noted, such a resource-based approach brings together a miscellaneous group of students reflecting different national definitions and policy concerns. Thus it was agreed to divide this group which into a tripartite taxonomy based on perceived causes of educational failure. These three agreed broad cross-national categories are referred to as

A, B and C – students with disabilities, learning difficulties and disadvantages respectively.

Students in cross-national category A (the 'disabilities' category) have clear organic bases for their difficulties in education. Students with disabilities or impairments viewed in medical terms as organic disorders attributable to organic pathologies (*e.g.* in relation to sensory, motor or neurological defects). The educational need is considered to arise primarily from problems attributable to these disabilities. (OECD 1998-2007)

Students in cross-national category B (the 'difficulties' category) have emotional and behaviour difficulties, or specific difficulties in learning and the educational need arises from problems in interaction between the student and the educational context.

Students in cross-national category C (the 'disadvantages' category) are in need of additional educational resources to compensate for problems due to aspects of their socio-economic, cultural and/or linguistic background (OECD 1998-2007).

Students with disabilities, learning difficulties and disadvantages are therefore a heterogeneous group which in some countries comprises only students with organic, physical and sensory disabilities, while in other countries it includes other groups such as socially and economically disadvantaged students and/or gifted and talented students.

By focusing on additional resources, the difficulties faced by students in accessing the curriculum for whatever reason are linked to the ability of schools to provide all students with the same chance to make progress in the education system and to achieve successfully in an appropriate learning environment (Ebersold and Evans, 2008).

This approach provides internationally comparable data that is easily understood and widely applicable.

Summary of current findings

National systems of education have developed procedures and practices for defining, identifying and resourcing students who have difficulties in accessing the curriculum. This is determined mainly by reference to national concepts and understanding based in cultural history and law making. International comparisons provide contrasts against which these assumptions can be re-analysed and re-conceptualised. The work carried out at OECD has shown that:

- The *classification* of students with disabilities, learning difficulties and disadvantages varies among countries; some OECD countries use 3 categories while others use 19.

- The *numbers* of students included vary widely, within comparable categories of disability. For instance, some countries identify and provide additional educational resources for ten times as many blind and partially sighted students as other countries (OECD 2004-2005).

- The *place* of education also varies substantially with some countries educating all students with disabilities in regular schools while others educate almost all of them in special schools. In some countries, children from socio-economically disadvantaged backgrounds are educated in segregated settings (*e.g.* the Czech Republic [OECD, 2004] and the Slovak Republic [OECD, 2005]) in contradistinction to most EU/OECD countries. Equity considerations lead to the position that students with disadvantages be educated in regular, mainstream schools rather than in separate institutions. The educational and social experiences of special schools and regular schools are different, and this could be inequitable in terms of students' access to post-compulsory education and the labour market.

- The large *gender* differences with the ratio of boys to girls identified for different programmes and given additional resources being in the order of 3 to 2. These differences should become a priority when countries examine the basis by which students are identified for different programmes, and examine the long-term consequences of participation in those programmes when they are provided in segregated facilities.

All of these factors raise questions about the educational practices of any one particular country and have policy implications, especially concerning the efficient and equitable use of funds. Thus the comparative context provides real added value by challenging national assumptions through evidence and data and in the context of global agreements. Furthermore, the appropriate education of students with disabilities, learning difficulties and disadvantages is a key factor in creating social cohesion and inclusion through the efficient use of education provision.

The electronic questionnaire

Data are provided from national authorities from datasets already gathered in countries for administrative purposes. An Electronic Questionnaire (EQ) was used to gather data on SENDDD and was designed to take account of the wide variety of national systems in use (The EQ is available for consultation from either OECD or CRELL). It comprises:

- Table 0 which requests information on any categories of students which are considered to fall within the resources definition and their classification into cross-national categories A, B or C.

- Table 1 which asks for information on the starting and ending ages of various stages of education.

- Table 2 which asks for information on the number of students with special educational needs in special schools, by level of education, by gender and by type of institutions (public and private), on numbers of classes and on the teaching staff.

- Table 3 which asks for information on the number of students with special needs in special classes, by level of education, by gender and by type of institutions (public and private), on numbers of classes and on the teaching staff.

- Table 4 which asks for information on the number of students with special needs in regular classes, by level of education, by gender and by type of institutions (public and private), and on numbers of classes.

- Table 6 which asks for information on all students enrolled in special educational programmes classified by age as well as on those not registered in the education system.

In the original data collection instrument, Table 5 requested data on programmes in national categories according to the ISCED definitions. Countries were unable to provide this information and as a result the table was dropped. To avoid confusion likely to be caused by renumbering the tables it was decided to keep the original numbering of the tables and simply omit Table 5.

The nature and sources of the database for this publication

Data are therefore available on the numbers of students with disabilities, learning difficulties and disadvantages receiving additional resources to make progress in their schooling, where they are educated (regular classes, special classes or special schools), number and sizes of schools and students/teacher ratios. Data are gathered on the total number of students in each phase of education (pre-primary through to upper secondary education including compulsory education) as well as gender and age breakdowns.

Within the framework of this joint study, returns of the Electronic Questionnaire were received from the following economies: Bulgaria, Croatia, Estonia, Kosovo, Latvia, Lithuania, Malta, Montenegro, Serbia, and Slovenia. Data gathered refer to the most recent available school year collection, *i.e.* 2005 with the exception of Estonia and Latvia for which data refer to school year 2006-2007. Annex 1 provides a list of EU and accession economies data returns.

These data were put into a database, using a methodology and a technology compatible with the general education statistics work undertaken by OECD and EUROSTAT. Data are collected every two years through an EQ which has been designed to be compatible with the UOE exercise. Data availability and corresponding OECD publications cover years 1999 (OECD, 2004), 2001 (OECD, 2005) and 2003 (OECD, 2007). Analysis of 2005 data is in progress. Qualitative data are gathered on legal frameworks and policies, and barriers to and facilitators of inclusion. Work has also been carried out on special needs students in PISA and with the study on Transition to Higher Education and Work new data at ISCED levels 4, 5 and 6 will be gathered on a small set of countries.

Data limitations

It is to be remarked that the data provided by national authorities are often scarce or incomplete. However, country experts recognise the importance of developing databases in this area and this book provides an account based on what is available. It is also recognised that there is a need for substantial investment and technical development in this field.

Despite increasing agreement about the cross-national definitions and growing adherence to these definitions among economies when allocating their individual national categories, divergences remain in harmonising international reporting of these data. Work to date has aimed at providing fuller data sets on all available national and cross-national categories.

Chapter descriptions

The present publication focuses on the data provided by the economies identified earlier for the academic year 2005 and presents analysis and discussions based on these data. In addition, it contains a chapter on the participation of students with disabilities, difficulties and disadvantages in PISA 2006. More specifically, this monograph is divided into two parts. The first part includes this introductory chapter and the following:

- Chapter 2, which provides a further analysis of the qualitative data.

- Chapter 3, which provides a comparative analysis of quantitative data based on categories used nationally to identify students who are in need of additional resources to help them access the curriculum.

- Chapter 4, which provides an analysis of quantitative data for cross-national categories A, B and C.

- Chapter 5, which provides an additional analysis of the quantitative data, including gender and age distributions.

The second part includes:

- Chapter 6, which provides a synthesis of country reports on statistics and indicators of students with special education needs and those at risk in South Eastern Europe, Malta and the Baltic States.

- Chapter 7, which presents a study that examined the participation of SEN students in PISA 2006.

- Chapter 8, which provides general conclusions and recommendations.

Symbols for missing data

The following symbols are employed in the tables and graphs to denote missing data:

a Data not applicable because the category does not apply.

m Data missing, not available.

n Magnitude is either negligible or zero.

x Data included in another category/column of the table.

Country codes

The following codes are used throughout this publication for participating economies:

Bosnia Herzegovina	BIH
Bulgaria	BGR
Croatia	HRV
Estonia	EST
Kosovo[2]	KSV
Latvia	LVA
Lithuania	LTU
Malta	MLT
Moldova	MDA
Montenegro	MNE
Romania	ROU
Serbia	SRB
Slovenia	SVN

---

[2] This terminology does not imply any legal position of the EC or OECD regarding the status of Kosovo.

References

Brighouse, M.H. (2000), *School choice and Social Justice*, Oxford: Oxford University Press.

Council of the European Union, Council Conclusions on a strategic framework for European co-operation in education and training, (ET 2020), 2941 Education, Youth and Culture Council meeting, Brussels, 12 May 2009.

Ebersold and Evans (2006), "A supply side approach for a resource based classification system" in Florian, L. and McLaughlin, M. J. (Eds.) (in press). *Dilemmas and Alternatives in the Classification of Children with Disabilities*: New Perspectives, Thousand Oaks, CA, Corwin Press.

European Commission (2006), "Communication from the Commission to the Council and to the European Parliament, Efficiency and Equity in the European Education and Training Systems.

Communication from the Commission of 20 Nov 2002. European Benchmarks in Education and Training: Follow-Up to the Lisbon European Council. [COM(2002)629final].

European Council 23-24 March 2006, Presidency Conclusions, par.23.

European Commission (2007), COM(2007) 61 final - Coherent Framework on Indicators and Benchmarks.

EC Official Journal C 162, 03/07/1990 P. 0002 - 0003

EC Council Decision 2001/903/EC of 3 December 2001.

EC Council Resolution 5165/03 e-Accessibility, 2003.

EC OJ C 134, 7.6.2003, p. 6.

EC OJ C 134, 7.6.2003, p. 7.

EC MEMO/06/321

Evans P. (2001), "Equity indicators based on the provision of supplemental resources for disabled and disadvantaged students" in W. Hutmacher, D. Cochrane and N. Bottani, *In Pursuit of Equity in Education*, Dordrech/Boston/London, Kluwer Academic Publishers.

Evans, P., Deluca, M. (2004), "Disabilities and gender in primary education", in *Education for All Global Monitoring Report*, UNESCO

OECD (1993), *Access, Participation and Equity*, OECD, Paris.

OECD (1995a), *Integrating Students with Special Needs into Mainstream Schools*, OECD, Paris.

OECD (1995b), *Our Children at Risk*, OECD, Paris.

OECD (1996*), Successful Services for our Children and Families at Risk*, OECD, Paris.

OECD (1998a), *Coordinating Services for Children and Youth at Risk. A World View*, OECD, Paris.

OECD (1998), *Education at a Glance – OECD Indicators*, Paris.

OECD (1999), I*nclusive Education at Work, Students with Disabilities in Mainstream Schools*, Paris, OECD.

OECD (2000), *Education at a Glance – OECD Indicators*, Paris.

OECD (2000), *Special Needs Education – Statistics and Indicators*, Paris.

OECD (2001) *Education at a Glance – OECD Indicators*, Paris.

OECD (2003), *Society at a Glance – OECD Social Indicators*, Paris.

OECD (2003), *Education Policy Analysis* – OECD, Paris.

OECD (2004), *Equity in Education - Students with Disabilities, Difficulties, and Disadvantages: Statistics and Indicators.* – OECD, Paris.

OECD (2005) *Students with Disabilities, Difficulties, and Disadvantages: Statistics and Indicators.* – OECD, Paris.

OECD (2006), *Education Policies for Students at Risk and those with Disabilities in South Eastern Europe* – OECD, Paris.

OECD (2007), *Students with Disabilities, Difficulties, and Disadvantages: Policies, Statistics and Indicators.* – OECD, Paris.

OECD (2007a) *Students with Disabilities, Difficulties, and Disadvantages: Statistics and Indicators in OAS countries.* – OECD/Edebe', Paris.

Rawls J. (1971), *A Theory of Justice*, Harvard University Press, Cambridge.

UN (1989), Convention on the Rights of the Child, NY.

UN (2006), Convention on the Rights of People with Disabilities, NY.

UNESCO (1997), International Standard Classification of Education - ISCED, Paris.

UNESCO (2006), *Education for All: Report*, UNESCO, Paris.

UNICEF (2004), *Innocenti Insight, Children and Disability in Transition in CEE/CIS and the Baltic States.*

World Education Forum (2000), The Dakar Framework for Action - Regional Framework for Action for the Americas. UNESCO, Paris

Chapter 2. Analysis of the Qualitative Data

This chapter summarises the qualitative data gathered by participating economies via an electronic questionnaire. Country experts reported on legal frameworks and on factors which facilitate or act as barriers to inclusion and equity as well as on definitions of special education for gathering statistics. This chapter also discusses the allocation of categories of students with disabilities, learning difficulties and disadvantages included in the resources definition to the tripartite taxonomy. This forms the basis for the subsequent analyses of this report.

Background

This chapter briefly summarises the qualitative data gathered by participating economies through the Electronic Questionnaire. Many of the issues are taken up in more detail in Chapter 6 where they have been amplified with additional material gathered through a more extensive survey. Eleven economies (Bosnia and Herzegovina (except Sarajevo Canton), Bulgaria, Croatia, Estonia, Kosovo, Latvia, Lithuania, Malta, Montenegro, Serbia and Slovenia) provided information via the Electronic Questionnaire on the following:

- Countries' definition of special education used for gathering educational statistics.

- The use of categories in gathering data in this field along with the names and definitions of the categories and whether or not they fall within the resources definition.

- Whether there are categories of students that fall within the resources definition but not within the national definition of special needs.

- How the categories fit into the cross-national categorisation A, B and C.

- Whether there is specific coverage of special educational needs in the current legislative framework and if so what it is.

- Factors considered to be facilitators of inclusion and equity, and factors acting as barriers to inclusion and equity.

The Electronic Questionnaire also asked for information on how planning decisions are made to ensure that students with special educational needs receive appropriate additional resources. This information was more difficult to obtain fully and is not reported here.

Legal frameworks

Country experts were asked to identify the specific coverage of special educational needs in the current legislative framework. In all economies surveyed, national laws foresee equal opportunities in education for all citizens regardless of their age, sex, religious or ethnic affiliations, health condition and financial circumstances. Both Governments and the Ministries of Education are typically responsible for ensuring equity in access to all forms of education for all.

Although all economies included in this study have ratified the Convention on the Rights of the Child and the 1994 Salamanca Action Framework only Croatia (15 August 2007) and Slovenia (24 April 2008) have ratified the UN Convention on the Rights of Persons with Disabilities and Bosnia and Herzegovina, Kosovo and Moldova have not yet signed it.

Whether there are more specific laws regarding special education needs varies from country to country. The majority of these economies underwent education reforms since the beginning of the 1990s. However, most of them reformed their education systems in the year 2000-2002. As explained later in Chapter 6, Ministries of Education are typically in charge although sometimes the responsibility is shared with the Ministry of Social Affairs, the Ministry of Labour and the Ministry of Health.

The most significant change in the legal frameworks is a move towards inclusion into regular education in an attempt to move away from the defectology[3] approach which still exists in many countries. Inclusion policies are driven by an agenda comprising human rights issues, equity, parental involvement and social cohesion. In addition, there is an increased understanding that students failing to make adequate progress in their learning is in large part a responsibility of the schooling system and cannot be viewed as being entirely due to problems existing within the student.

In some economies the move towards inclusive education has generated adapted educational curricula and inclusive education for students with disabilities, learning difficulties and disadvantages.

Even though a legislative framework may be in place there are many difficulties in implementation, such as conceptual divergences *vis-à-vis* integration and inclusion, privileged use of special provision, Roma misplacement and drop-out, poor pre-school attendance, poor early intervention, inadequate teacher training, low parents participation, lack of funding, etc.

Facilitators and barriers of equity and inclusive education

Country experts were asked to identify characteristics of their educational systems which they believe act as either facilitators or barriers to equity and inclusive education.

Universal entitlement, rights and positive legal frameworks were viewed as positive features for inclusion. Other facilitators reported were accessibility of schools, reform implementation *vis-à-vis* curricula development, pedagogy and teacher training, individualised teaching programmes, adequate and flexible funding and co-ordination

---

[3] Defectology is a system of diagnosing and treating children with disabilities that was developed in the Soviet Union and still used widely in CIS countries. It emphasises the identification and classification of children with disabilities and their education and health care in segregated provision specifically tailored for their needs.

among responsible authorities and good support systems such as transportation, and the promotion of a positive attitude towards inclusion among teacher unions and the availability of staff. The existence of diversity in the population was also seen as a positive attribute fostering good attitudes towards inclusion.

Parents are cited as the most powerful advocates for their children with disabilities and in some economies they created associations for mutual support and lobbying. Typically, parents can participate in the process of diagnostic evaluation of disability. Parents' involvement is reported as being crucial in the choice of educational programmes for students with disabilities, learning difficulties and disadvantages. Other economies reported low parental participation and this is due to the fact that they feel isolated socially and are left with no support from trained teachers or specialists. Some parents spend time in the class with their children and/or have to take time off work in order to take their children to school.

Countries reported that variations between local administrations were too great and there were often negative attitudes held by a wide range of persons towards special education and inclusion. Teaching staff were inadequately trained to work with SENDDD students and this was not helped by an ageing teaching population. Assistants were often too rigid about who they worked with in inclusive settings. The lack of appropriate teaching and learning resources were considered as a major barrier to equity and inclusive education. Also poor monitoring of progress was reported, as well as a lack of transition arrangements at all levels and counselling.

Limited funding at local and school levels is also seen as a major barrier for the advancement of equity and inclusion in educational systems. In Croatia, however, national budget funds were guaranteed to reach 'the network of schools without barriers' in every county.

The structural barriers of examination arrangements and many school facilities and class size were cited as limiting effective inclusive strategies.

A lack of standardised information and co-ordination in data gathering was reported. While data exist about students in special schools and to some extent about students in special classes in regular schools, it is less clear how many students with disabilities, learning difficulties and disadvantages in receipt of additional resources to make progress in their schooling there are in mainstream education. This will be examined in more depth in Chapters 3, 4 and 5.

Substantial investment and technical development in this area was cited as needed in order to identify the number of invisible children, that is children without papers, birth certificates as well as those who are kept out of schools by families for various reasons. Many are likely to be disabled and in need of additional resources, equipment, pedagogical aids and adaptations in order to access the curriculum.

Definition of special education for gathering statistics

Based on the information provided by country experts, the definitions of special education for the purposes of gathering national statistics may be grouped into three basic patterns.

Table 2.1 **Classification of nationally gathered categories used in collecting data within the national definition of special educational needs**

Countries/Patterns	Disability categories only	Disability categories plus disadvantaged students	Disability categories plus gifted and talented students
Bosnia and Herzegovina		✓ [1]	
Bulgaria		✓ [1]	
Croatia		✓ [1]	
Estonia		✓ [1]	
Kosovo	✓		
Latvia		✓	
Lithuania	✓		
Malta	✓		
Moldova	✓		
Montenegro		✓ [1]	
Romania	✓		
Serbia	✓ [1]		
Slovenia			✓

Note: [1] Includes learning difficulties linked to linguistic barriers or disadvantage associated with ethnic groupings.

The data summarised in Table 2.1 illustrate that almost all economies collect data via disability categories, but the term disability often has different meanings in different countries. Secondly, there are some countries, *e.g.* Bulgaria, Croatia, Estonia, Latvia, Montenegro, Serbia, which also include disadvantaged students. Additionally, some countries (*e.g.* Croatia, Estonia, Montenegro, and Serbia) include children with a foreign first language within these categories whilst others do not. Thirdly, some countries, *e.g.* Slovenia, also include gifted and talented students.

The use of categories in gathering data in this field

Country experts were asked to identify the use of categories in gathering data in this field along with the names and definitions of the categories and whether or not they fall within the resources definition.

The term 'special educational needs' covers an array of problems from those related to particular impairments to those related to learning and behavioural difficulties experienced by some learners compared to other similar learners. The number of categories of special need varies between economies from 3 to 10. Many economies use levels of severity from mild to severe (sometimes referred to as 'hard') to differentiate within categories. The categories always include sensory impairments (vision and hearing) and physical impairments. Most economies also include cognitive impairments, but these are described in different ways and may or may not include specific difficulties in learning such as dyslexia. Some have emotional, social and behavioural difficulties as a single category; others see them as separate and distinctive. Some economies have a category of communication disorders, which may or may not include speech and language difficulties. Sometimes autism is seen as a communication disorder. In South Eastern Europe, Malta and the Baltic States, the term 'special needs' is often considered to mean children with physical or mental disabilities.

The data show that most economies gather data by means of categories and they were invited to provide the names of the categories and their definitions. Most economies were able to provide definitions and the outcomes are provided in full in Table 2.2 which reveals the complexity of the various arrangements. In this table, the national categories have been allocated to cross-national categories A, B and C according to the classification provided by economies themselves as requested and as discussed in meetings of country experts.

Definitions of the categories are also provided where available. In addition, those categories which receive additional resources but which are not part of the national special needs category system are included in the table. A detailed quantitative analysis of data based on national categories is provided in Chapter 3.

Categories of students that fall within the resources but not the national definition of special needs

Some economies report having categories which receive additional resources but which lie outside their national definition of special needs (Croatia, Latvia, Malta, Montenegro and Serbia). These tend to cover disadvantaged students, students from ethnic minorities and those with short term learning problems or specific learning difficulties. However, some countries (*e.g.* Estonia) also include gifted and talented students.

The tripartite cross-national classification

Country experts were asked to carry out the task of re-classifying their categories, both national and resource-based, according to the cross-national tripartite model described in Chapter 1. The allocation of national categories to cross-national categories was discussed and agreed upon at the various CRELL/OECD meetings held regularly during the time of the study and results are summarised in Table 2.2 below and in Annex 2. Table 2.2 and Annex 2 reveal that economies use categories to classify their special needs population for the purposes of statistical data gathering. In terms of national categories, *i.e.* excluding those that additionally fall into the resources definition, they vary in number between 7 (Malta) and 12 (Montenegro).

Although the categories used cover broadly similar conditions, in many economies actual definitions in use render comparisons difficult. For instance, with regard to students with learning difficulties, it is not always possible to distinguish between students with severe learning difficulties, moderate learning difficulties, mild learning difficulties and learning disabilities as was also the case for OECD countries. Another difference is that some OECD countries gather data on students who are blind or have partial sight separately, whereas these target countries group them together, and similarly for those who are deaf or have partial hearing impairments. Almost all countries reported students with emotional and behavioural problems in contrast to OECD countries where many countries did not use this category.

Having detailed definitions for most national categories has increased the reliability of their allocation to cross-national categories A, B and C, since the understanding of the wide variety of national category names is facilitated. In South Eastern Europe, the Baltic States and Malta cross-national category A/Disabilities is the most widely used for the collection of data. All economies surveyed (except Kosovo, Malta, Slovenia) allocated national categories to cross-national category C/Disadvantages. All countries and economies allocated categories of students with emotional and behavioural problems and learning difficulties to cross-national category B/Difficulties.

However, some anomalies still remained, and this led to discussions with country experts and subsequent re-allocation of some national categories within the tripartite categorisation system.

Table 2.2 **Allocation of categories of students with disabilities, learning difficulties and disadvantages (included in the resources definition) to cross-national categories A, B and C**

Note: A fuller description of each of the categories as supplied by country representatives is provided in Annex 2.

BOSNIA AND HERZEGOVINA

Cross-National Category A

1. Mild mental retardation
2. Moderate mental retardation
3. Severe mental retardation
4. Profound mental retardation
5. Autism
6. Motor difficulties and chronic diseases
7. Blindness and low vision
8. Deafness and hearing impairments
9. Combined difficulties
10. Down's syndrome
11. Speech and language difficulties

Cross-National Category B

12. Learning difficulties
13. Attention Deficit Hyperactivity Disorder (ADHD)

Cross-National Category C

14. Difficulties caused by socio-economic, cultural deprivation and/or caused by linguistic factors

BULGARIA

Cross-National Category A

1. Students with mental retardation
2. Students with hearing impairments
3. Students with visual impairments
4. Students with speech-language disorders
5. Students with physical impairments
7. Students with multiple disorders
8. Students with autism

Cross-National Category B

6. Students with learning difficulties
9. Students with psychological disorders

Cross-National Category C

10. Students with other difficulties due to social reasons

CROATIA

Cross-National Category A

1. Visual impairment
2. Hearing impairment
4. Physical disability
5. Mental retardation
6. Organic conditioned behaviour dysfunctions
7. Autism
8. Other visual impairment
11. Health problems

Cross-National Category B

3. Dysfunctions of speaking and voice communication (speech and language disabilities)
9. Specific learning difficulties/Other dysfunctions of speaking and voice communication
10. Reduced cognitive function/Remedial Education
12. Behaviour problems
13. Hyperactivity and attention deficit
14. Addictions

Cross-National Category C

15. Other difficulties/disadvantages
16. Institutional accommodations
17. Family problems
18. Language dysfunctions (Second language)

ESTONIA

Cross-National Category A

1. Students with intellectual disability
4. Students with mental health problems
5. Students with multiple disabilities
6. Students with hearing impairment
7. Students with visual impairment
8. Students with speech impairment
9. Students with physical disabilities
11. Students with chronic and progressive diseases

Cross-National Category B

2. Students with learning difficulties
3. Students with specific learning difficulties
10. Students with behavioural difficulties
12. Students with temporary learning difficulties
15. Gifted students (not applicable)

Cross-National Category C

13. Students with accommodation difficulties
14. Immigrant students

KOSOVO (UNMIK – PISG)

Cross-National Category A

1. Intellectual impairment
2. Hearing impairment
3. Visual impairment
4. Physical impairment
5. Multiple impairments
6. Autism

Cross-National Category B

7. Emotional disorders

LATVIA

Cross-National Category A

1. Disabilities of mental development (mental retardation)
3. Visual impairments
4. Hearing impairments
5. Physical disabilities
7. Mental health disorders
8. Chronic health problems (somatic illnesses)

Cross-National Category B

2. Learning disabilities
6. Speech and language disabilities
10. Pedagogical correction/ Remedial Teaching

Cross-National Category C

9. Disadvantaged background

LITHUANIA

Cross-National Category A

1. Intellectual disorders
5. Hearing disorders
6. Visual disorders
7. Movement disorders
8. Somatic and neurological disorders
9. Complex disorders

Cross-National Category B

2. Specific learning difficulties
3. Emotional, behaviour and socialization disorders
4. Speech and other communication disorders

Cross-National Category C

10. Other disorders

MALTA

Cross-National Category A

1. Intellectual Disability
4. Communication Difficulty
5. Sensory Difficulties
6. Physical Disability
7. Multiple Disability

Cross-National Category B

2. Specific Learning Difficulty
3. Emotional and Behavioural Difficulty

MOLDOVA

NOT PROVIDED

MONTENEGRO

Cross-National Category A

1. Children with physical disabilities
2. Children with intellectual disabilities
3. Children with visual impairments
4. Children with hearing impairments
5. Children with speech difficulties
6. Children with hard chronically diseases
7. Children with combined difficulties
8. Children with long-term diseases

Cross-National Category B

9. Children with behavioural problems
10. Children with emotional problems
11. Children with learning disabilities

Cross-National Category C

12. Social disadvantages

ROMANIA

NOT PROVIDED

SERBIA

Cross-National Category A

1. Bodily invalid children
2. Blind students
3. Deaf students
4. Mentally retarded children
5. Pupils at hospital/home treatment
9. Autism

Cross-National Category B

6. Writing difficulties
7. Reading difficulties
8. Hyperkinetic syndrome

Cross-National Category C

10. Difficulties caused by linguistic and cultural deprivation and socio-economic factors

---

SLOVENIA

Cross-National Category A

1. Children with a mild mental disability
2. Children with a moderate, severe and profound mental disability
3. Children with visual impairments and blind
4. Children with hearing impairments and deaf
5. Children with speech and language disorders
6. Children with physical disabilities
7. Children with long term illness
8. Children with deficits in individual areas of learning (Pupils with severe specific learning disability)
12. Children with boundary intelligence[4]

Cross-National Category B

9. Children with behavioural or emotional disorders
10. Pupils with learning difficulties
11. Gifted and talented (not applicable)

Concluding comments

The qualitative data gathered during the study reveal the great national interest in this area as laws, policies and educational provision are adjusted to meet the needs of students who are failing in the regular system. Factors identified as facilitators for, or barriers to equity and inclusion cover a whole range of issues which make a substantial agenda for reform. They are: legal frameworks, funding models, assessment arrangements, school structure, class size, individual teaching programmes, involvement of additional teachers and aids, teacher training, parental involvement and co-operation with other services.

The allocation of national categories to the cross-national categories A, B and C was carried out successfully and thus supports the method developed for OECD countries.

The discussion above on the results of the findings on national categories and on the way they are allocated to the tripartite categorisation system strongly supports the rationale of the present study. That is, if meaningful international comparisons are to be made, a method such as the one developed here, which includes all children receiving additional resources and their assignment into straightforward and operationally defined categories, substantially simplifies the situation and improves the possibility of making policy-relevant decisions based on internationally valid comparisons.

The quantitative data gathered by means of the electronic questionnaire are examined in detail in the next chapters.

---

[4] As of March 2006 this category is no longer used.

References

OECD (2005), *Students with Disabilities, Learning Difficulties and Disadvantages: Statistics and Indicators*, Paris, OECD.

OECD (2006), *Education Policies for Students at Risk and those with Disabilities in South Eastern Europe*, Paris, OECD.

OECD findings from the Follow-Up Visits October 2006-January 2007 (OECD, EDU/EDPC(2007)/21).

OECD (2007), *Students with Disabilities, Learning Difficulties and Disadvantages: Policies, Statistics and Indicators*, Paris, OECD.

OECD (2007), *Students with Disabilities, Learning Difficulties and Disadvantages: Statistics and Indicators in OAS Countries*, Paris, OECD/Edebe.

Chapter 3. Analysis of the Quantitative Data Based on Categories Used Nationally

This chapter analyses the data based on the national categories used to provide additional resources for students who have difficulties in accessing the curriculum, as supplied by participating economies. It looks at the proportions registered in education statistics in the compulsory phase of education, by individual category of disability, learning difficulty or disadvantage and by location of education (special schools, special classes and regular classes).

Background

This chapter analyses the data provided by country representatives in Tables 2, 3 and 4 of the electronic questionnaire (covering special schools, special classes and regular classes respectively) by national categories of disability, learning difficulty and disadvantage based on the resources definition given in Chapter 1. This analysis follows a similar format to that in the corresponding chapter in the earlier publication *Students with Disabilities, Learning Difficulties and Disadvantages: Policies, Statistics and Indicators* (OECD, 2007).

The data are broken down by categories and presented as proportions of the total numbers of students in compulsory education, where typically the most complete information is reported. Annex 3 provides information on starting and ending ages of the period of compulsory education, by country. In addition, information is provided on the setting or location of these students' education, *i.e.* in regular classes, special classes or special schools, expressed as proportions of the total numbers of students in that category in the particular location.

The data in this chapter have been assembled in the full knowledge of the difficulty of making international comparisons on the basis of national categories. However, the analysis is carried out in order to keep touch with the basic data in the form in which they were presented, using terminology that many readers would follow more readily and to provide the context for comparisons made through cross-national categories A, B and C in Chapter 4. The method used to make the comparisons is outlined below. Table 2.2 in the previous chapter provides background information revealing the inherent difficulty in making international comparisons. Although all countries use categorical models they are not used in a uniform way among countries. Furthermore, the definitions of the categories, when available, vary among countries. It is of course partly for these reasons that the resources model and the cross-national categorisation system have been developed.

Methodology

In order to make the comparisons across the categories provided by participating economies, it is necessary to bring together the different national frameworks that exist. In order to do this, the definitions of the categories were carefully scrutinised and brought together according to the structure of the matrix given in Table 3.1. The data classification displayed in this matrix was used to construct the comparative charts given in the chapter. For example, columns 2 and 3 show national categories covering students who have visual or hearing impairments. The data for Malta for example shows a "5x" in column 2 and a "5x" in column 3. The "5" refers to the national category covering students who have visual or hearing impairments (see Table 3.2) and the "x" indicates that students with hearing impairments are also included in the category "visual impairments". This means that data cannot be shown separately for these two categories.[5] This is in contrast, for instance, to Bulgaria where the data on students with hearing impairments are contained in their national category 2 and data for students with visual impairments in their national category 3. Comparative figures are only presented if data are available for three or more countries.

Data on individual categories

Table 3.1 provides an overview of the data availability for each of the participating economies in terms of the 15 internationally comparable categories. As countries differ in the ways they categorise different types of disabilities, difficulties and disadvantages, many cells in the matrix are blank.

In what follows, data for each category are presented in two types of figure: firstly, in terms of the numbers of students in the category receiving additional resources to access the curriculum across the period of compulsory education as a proportion of the total number of students in compulsory education. The numbers in these figures can therefore be seen as a proxy for the prevalence rate of each of these categories in each country. The second type of figure for each category focuses on where these students are educated: in regular classes, special classes or special schools. The figures show the proportion of students in each category receiving additional resources in each of the three settings.

In all figures, countries are ranked in ascending order either in terms of overall percentages or descending order in terms of their distribution in regular classes.

The categories concerning blind and partially sighted students are presented together since the majority of countries do not keep separate data for the two individual categories. This also applies for the data on partially hearing and deaf students, and for those with severe and moderate learning problems. Data on gifted and talented students are not analysed because the educational issues and challenges regarding gifted and talented children would appear to be very different from those faced by students with disabilities, learning difficulties and disadvantages.

The figures are based on full-time study. Data refer to school year 2005, with the exception of Estonia, where data cover the period 2006. Some figures include an OECD

---

[5] Malta has a category 'Sensory Difficulties' which includes visual and hearing impairment and 'other' conditions – see Table 2.2.

median which refers to data from school year 2003. The figures are based on both public and private institutions.

Table 3.1 **Distribution of 15 internationally comparable categories by country**

	Visual impairment/Blindness	Hearing impairment/Deafness	Emotional, behavioural difficulties	Mild, moderate and/or severe learning problems	Light learning problems (eg IQ 70-85)	Physical disabilities	Combinatorial disabilities	Specific learning difficulties	Speech and language problems	Hospital/Chronic diseases	Autism	Second language	Residential provision	Remedial teaching / Pedagogical correction	Disadvantaged students
Bosnia and Herzegovina*	7	8	13	1, 2, 3, 4, 10		6	9	12	11		5			14x	14x
Bulgaria	3	2	9	1		5	7	6	4	8					10
Croatia	1, 8	2	12, 13, 14	5		4			3, 9	11	7	18	16	10	15, 17
Estonia	7	6	10	1, 4x	2	9	5	3	8	11	4x	14	13	12	
Kosovo	3	2	7	1		4	5				6				
Latvia	3	4		1, 7		5		2	6	8				10	9
Lithuania	6	5	3	1		7	9	2	4	8				10	
Malta	5x	5x	3	1		6	7	2	4x		4x				
Montenegro	3	4	9, 10	2		1	7	11	5	6, 8		12x			12x
Serbia	2	3	8, 9	4		1			6, 7		5	9	10		
Slovenia	3	4	9	1, 2	10x, 12x	6		8	5	7				10x	

Note: * Bosnia and Herzegovina: Data are available for all cantons except Sarajevo canton.

From the point of view of making international comparisons, inspection of Table 3.1 reveals that such comparisons are difficult due to the inconsistent use of categories among the various economies. Only blind and partially sighted, deaf and partially hearing, and physical disabilities are used by all countries. The remaining categories are used to varying degrees. Of the 15 categories given in Table 3.1, 12 are discussed in greater detail in the following sections. OECD median values are provided where four or more countries have comparable data.

It should be noted that every effort has been made to avoid double counting. In some cases, proportions may be underestimated because of missing data.

Description by category

Blind and partially sighted

The statistics on the categories covering blind and partially sighted students are brought together as a single category. As can be seen from Figure 3.1 the proportion of blind and partially sighted students receiving additional resources is around the OECD median – 0.05% – in many of the economies presented. The extremes are Serbia with 1.13% and Estonia with 0.03%.

Figure 3.1 **Numbers of blind and partially sighted students receiving additional resources as a percentage of all students in compulsory education**

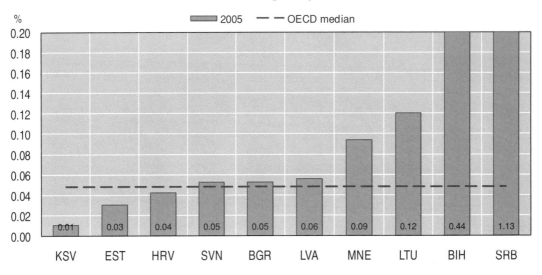

Notes: Kosovo: there are students with special needs who are provided with additional resources in regular classes but the data are not available.
Serbia: this percentage includes students who wear glasses.

Figure 3.2 shows where these students are educated (regular classes, special classes or special schools). It shows that five countries educate 60% or more of these students in regular classes (Croatia, Lithuania, Montenegro, Serbia and Slovenia). Bulgaria and Estonia educate respectively 70% and 77% of them in segregated settings, while in Latvia students with visual impairments are almost all in special schools.

Figure 3.2 **Percentages of blind and partially sighted students receiving additional resources in compulsory education by location**

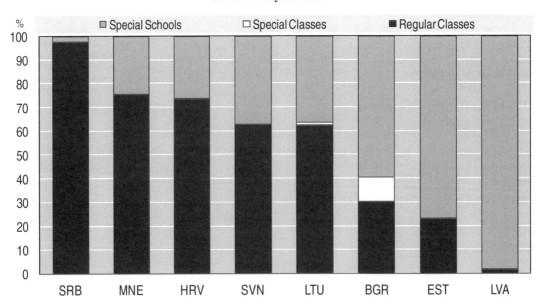

Deaf and partially hearing

As for blind and partially sighted students, the statistics gathered on categories covering deaf and partially hearing pupils are treated as a single data category in all the economies covered and this method is adopted here.

As can be seen from Figure 3.3, the proportion of deaf and partially hearing students registered in educational statistics varies from country to country. The lowest percentage is in Bulgaria with 0.05%, and the highest in Croatia, Latvia, Lithuania and Serbia, between 0.16% and 0.23%. Bosnia and Herzegovina and Montenegro are close to the OECD median of 0.09%.

Figure 3.3 **Numbers of deaf and partially hearing students by country, as a percentage of all students in compulsory education**

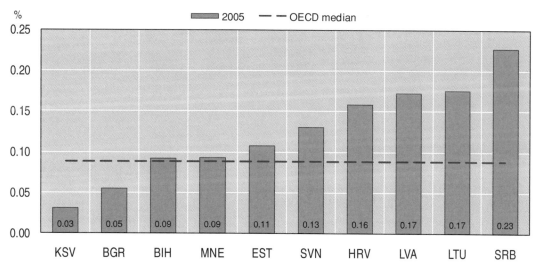

Note: Kosovo: there are students with special needs who are provided with additional resources in regular classes but the data are not available.

Figure 3.4 shows how variable the placement of these students is among countries. All three arrangements for educating students with hearing impairments are found, from 80% in regular classes in Serbia and Slovenia to 95% in special schools in Latvia. Bulgaria makes the most extensive use of special classes for these students (18%) but it should be noted that it identifies a very low number of students – 0.05%, well below the OECD median of 0.09%.

Figure 3.4 **Percentages of deaf and partially hearing students receiving additional resources in compulsory education by location**

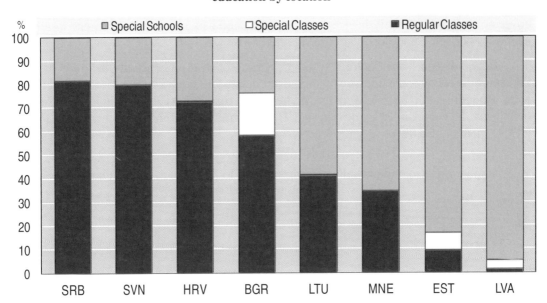

Emotional and/or behavioural difficulties

As can be seen from Figure 3.5 the proportion of students with emotional and behavioural difficulties who receive additional resources varies substantially from country to country. Croatia (3.13%) stands out from the others. Malta, Estonia and Montenegro range between 0.7% and 0.9%. Lithuania is in line with the OECD median of 0.38%. The remaining three countries, Slovenia, Bulgaria and Serbia, are below it.

Figure 3.5 **Numbers of students with emotional and/or behavioural difficulties by country, as a percentage of all students in compulsory education**

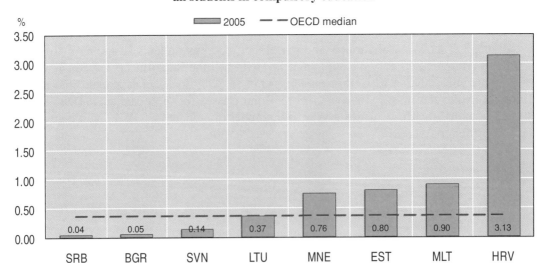

Figure 3.6 shows the variety of placements offered to these students. The majority of the students with emotional and behavioural difficulties are being educated in regular

classes. This is the situation in all countries except in Estonia where two thirds of them are in special classes. In Croatia and Serbia they are all or almost all included in regular classes.

It is of interest to note that given the apparent rise in the numbers of students described as having behaviour difficulties, not all countries use such a category (OECD, 2007). For those which do, there is evidence for a greater use of special classes and regular classes than in the two preceding clusters of categories.

Figure 3.6 **Percentages of students with emotional and/or behavioural difficulties receiving additional resources in compulsory education by location**

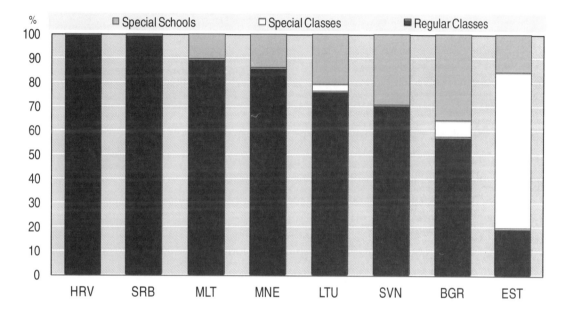

Physical disability

It is readily observable from Figure 3.7 that there is great variation in the proportion of students with physical disabilities receiving additional resources in all participating economies. Four countries, Latvia (0.48%), Malta (0.40%), Lithuania (0.38%) and Croatia (0.36%) have proportions well above the OECD median, Slovenia and Estonia are around the OECD median of 0.17%, and in Bulgaria and Montenegro the numbers are well below it.

Figure 3.7 **Numbers of students with physical disabilities by country as a percentage of all students in compulsory education**

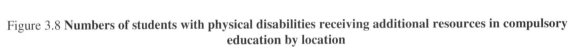

Notes: Kosovo: there are students with special needs who are provided with additional resources in regular classes but the data are not available.
Latvia: this percentage includes students with scoliosis

Figure 3.8 shows how variable the placement of these students is among countries. In seven countries, 60% or more of students with physical disabilities are placed in regular classes. Estonia and Latvia are the exceptions as they integrate less than 5% in regular classes. Of the five countries which use all three locations, regular classes, special classes and special schools, Latvia and, to a lesser extent, Bulgaria stand out making large use of special classes, with 37% and 18%, respectively.

Figure 3.8 **Numbers of students with physical disabilities receiving additional resources in compulsory education by location**

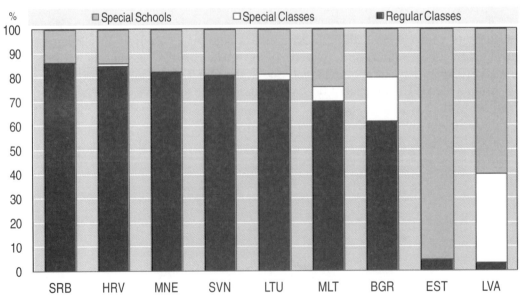

Speech and language problems

As can be seen from Figure 3.9, the percentages of students registered with speech and language problems also vary substantially from country to country. They range from 0.04% in Bosnia and Herzegovina to just over 7% in Lithuania. Croatia also shows a high percentage (2%). The other countries stand around the OECD median of 0.21%, Latvia and Slovenia being above it, and Bosnia and Herzegovina, Bulgaria, Estonia and Montenegro below it.

Figure 3.9 **Numbers of students with speech and language problems by country, as a percentage of all students in compulsory education**

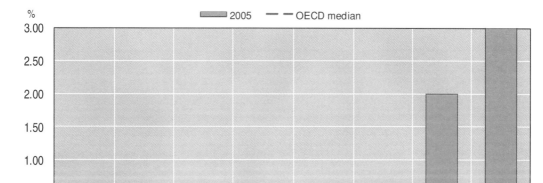

Figure 3.10 shows where these students are being educated (regular classes, special classes or special schools). In five of the seven countries, the majority of these students are in regular classes. In Lithuania, Croatia and Montenegro almost all students with speech and language problems are integrated in regular schools. In Estonia and Latvia, less than 2% are in regular classes.

Figure 3.10 **Percentages of students with speech and language problems receiving additional resources in compulsory education by location**

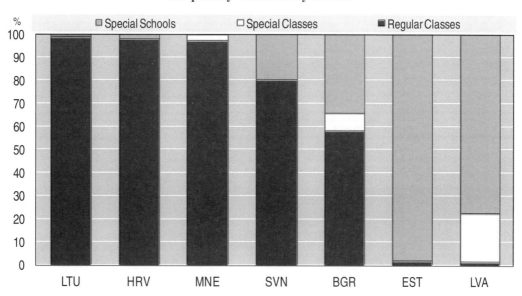

Hospital/Long term sickness

As can be seen from Figure 3.11, the percentage of students registered as receiving education while hospitalised or in long-term sickness ranges from 0.15% in Slovenia to 0.83% in Croatia. All countries presented here report numbers above the OECD median – 0.09%, but among OECD countries, in 2003, the Czech Republic and the Slovak Republic reported 0.52% and 0.39% respectively.

Figure 3.11 **Numbers of students in hospital by location as a percentage of all students in compulsory education**

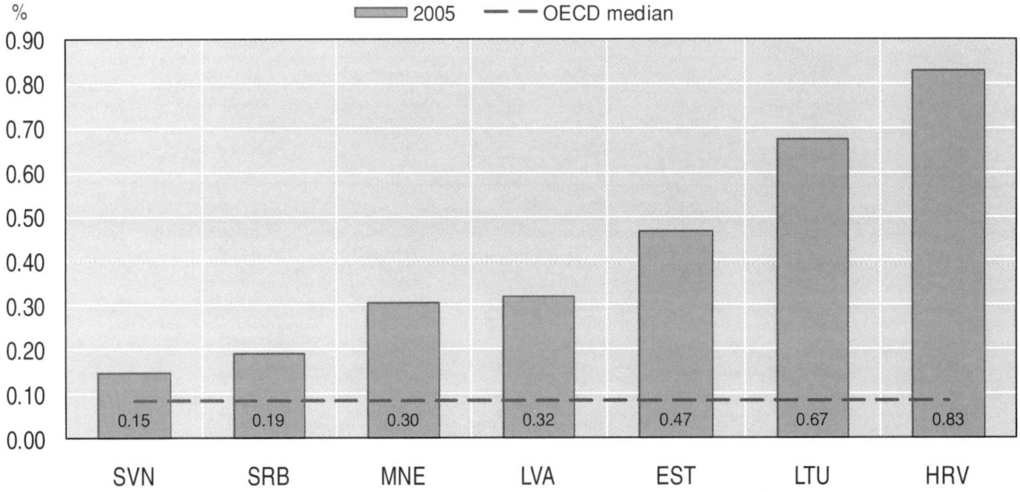

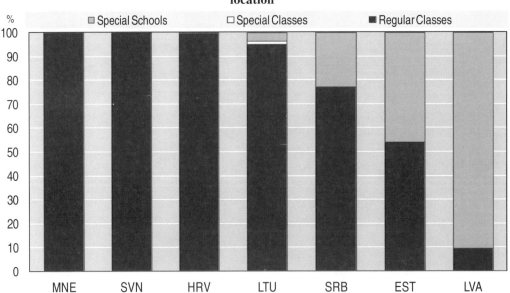

There appears to be less variation among countries for this category than for other categories. Figure 3.12 shows in which type of school the students in hospital or in long-term sickness are registered (mostly in regular classes or special schools). In four countries (Montenegro, Slovenia, Croatia and Lithuania) they are almost all registered in regular classes. In Latvia, only 9.4% of these students are registered in regular classes.

Figure 3.12 **Percentages of students in hospital receiving additional resources in compulsory education by location**

Combinatorial disabilities

Combinatorial disabilities is a term that has been coined by the OECD Secretariat to avoid the confusion in an earlier monograph (OECD, 2000) over the use of the term "multiple disability" which in the United States is a legally defined category but which is too precisely defined to cover the range of students included in the "combinatorial" category used here.

Figure 3.13 shows that again the proportions of students in this category vary substantially from country to country. Even leaving Lithuania aside given the high percentage (1.46%), the percentages still vary substantially ranging from 0.37% in Malta to 0.04% in Montenegro.

Figure 3.13 **Numbers of students with combinatorial disabilities by country, as % of all students in compulsory education**

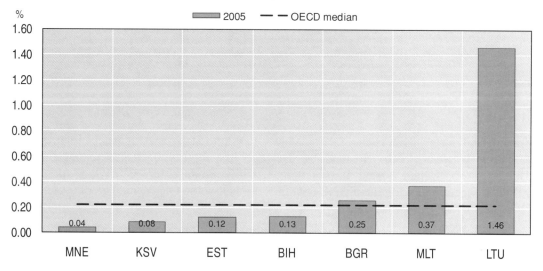

Note: Kosovo: there are students with special needs who are provided with additional resources in regular classes but the data are not available.

Figure 3.14 illustrates clearly the variability in placement among countries. All types of arrangements can be found among the five countries for which data are available. Lithuania and Malta use regular classes for more than 70% of these students. Montenegro uses this provision for 60% of students, but also makes a large use of special classes (30%). In Bulgaria, two thirds of students with combinatorial disabilities are placed in segregated settings, and in Estonia 98% are in special schools.

Figure 3.14 **Percentages of students with combinatorial disabilities receiving additional resources in compulsory education by location**

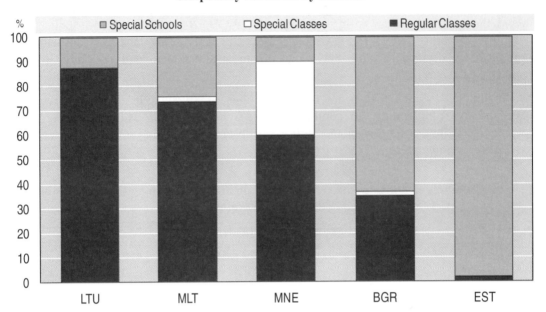

Autism

Four countries use this as a clear category to gather statistics. Figure 3.15 shows the variation between them. Bosnia and Herzegovina reports 0.01%, Croatia, 0.02%, Bulgaria, 0.03% and Serbia indicates that 0.04% students are receiving additional resources specifically for autism. All countries are below the OECD median of 0.043%.

Figure 3.15 **Numbers of students with autism by country as a percentage of all students in compulsory education**

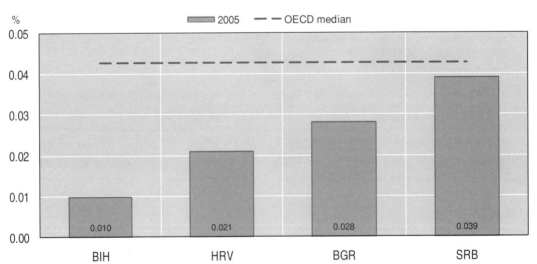

Figure 3.16 shows where these students are being educated. The three countries for which data are available show a different pattern in the provision. Bulgaria makes use of all types of setting, while Croatia privileges special schools (82%) and Serbia privileges regular classes.

Figure 3.16 **Percentages of students with autism receiving additional resources in compulsory education by location**

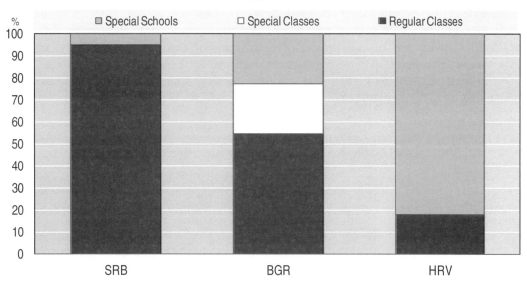

Mild, moderate and/or severe learning problems

Figure 3.17 shows the proportions of resourced students with mild, moderate and/or severe learning problems by country. Three groups of economies can be formed. Estonia and Latvia are in a first group with very high percentages, 2.72% and 2.96%, respectively. In a second group, Croatia, Malta, Lithuania, Slovenia and Serbia report percentages between 1.14% and 1.58%. Bulgaria, Montenegro, and Bosnia and Herzegovina are in a third group with low percentages between 0.54% and 0.39%. For comparability reasons, it was decided not to compare this group of categories with the OECD median.

Figure 3.17 **Numbers of students with mild, moderate and/or severe and/or learning problems by country, as a percentage of all students in compulsory education**

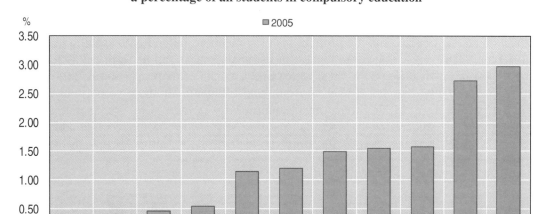

Notes: Kosovo: there are students with special needs who are provided with additional resources in regular classes but the data are not available.

Estonia: this percentage includes students in category "autism".

Figure 3.18 shows where these students are being educated (regular classes, special classes or special schools). There is no overall pattern in provision. Countries vary to a large extent over where they educate students. In Slovenia, all the students with mild, moderate and/or severe learning problems are educated in special schools. All other economies make use of the three different types of settings, but in very variable proportions. The share of these students being placed in segregated settings ranges from 10% in Malta to 90% in Latvia. The countries making broad use of special classes are Montenegro (25%), Croatia (15%), Estonia (11%) and Latvia (8%).

Figure 3.18 **Percentages of students with mild, moderate and/or severe and/or learning problems receiving additional resources in compulsory education by location**

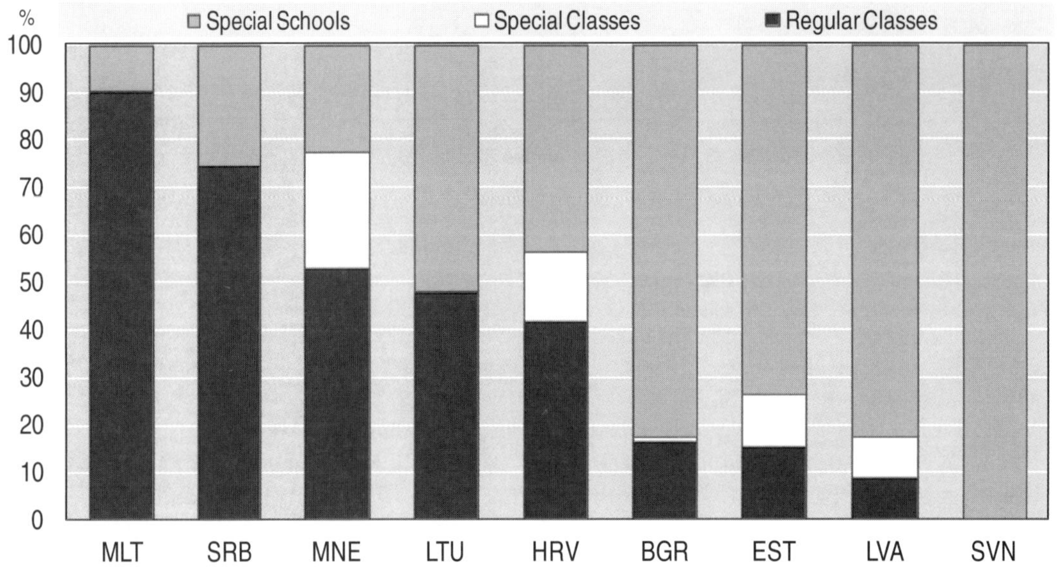

Specific learning difficulties

Figure 3.19 shows that, as for many of the other categories, there is very substantial variation among countries in the proportions of students resourced with specific learning difficulties. This proportion is the highest in Estonia (4.08%) and in Serbia (3.59%); and the lowest is in Malta (0.06%). In Slovenia and Lithuania this proportion is 2.09% and 1.70% respectively. Estonia, Serbia, Slovenia and Lithuania all show proportions above the OECD median. In the four other countries for which data are available, the percentages of students with specific learning difficulties who receive additional resources range between 0.16% for Bulgaria to 0.49% for Latvia, below the OECD median of 1.41%.

Figure 3.19 **Numbers of students with specific learning difficulties by country, as a percentage of all students in compulsory education**

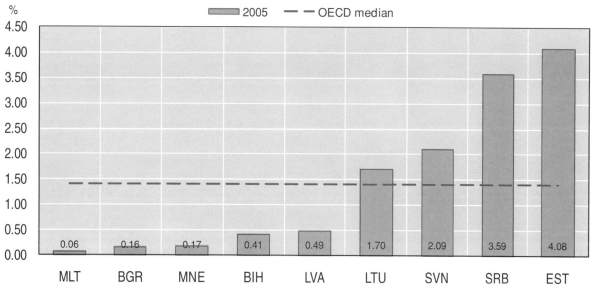

Figure 3.20 shows where these students are being educated (regular classes, special classes or special schools). In six of the countries presented (Estonia, Malta, Serbia, Slovenia, Montenegro, and Lithuania), the vast majority or the whole of these students are integrated in regular classes. The exceptions are Latvia, which makes extensive use of segregated settings for this type of students (47.2% in special schools and 30.0% in special classes); and to a lesser extent, Bulgaria (16.9% and 6.8%).

Figure 3.20 **Numbers of students with specific learning difficulties by location and by country, as a percentage of all students with specific learning difficulties in primary and lower secondary education**

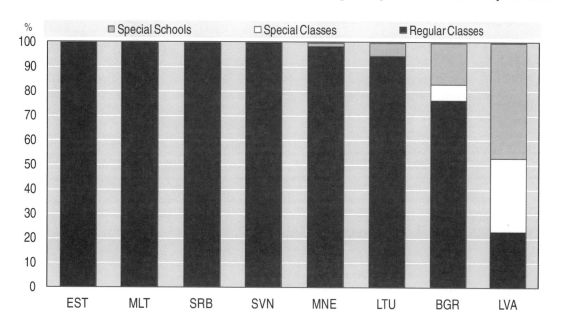

Categories related to disadvantage

The analysis presented in the following section is based on data on national categories related to disadvantage where common categories could be provided for making international comparisons. Only two such categories emerged: students with a second language and disadvantaged students.

Second language

Figure 3.21 shows the percentages of second language students by country as a percentage of all students in compulsory education and their distribution by place of education. Three countries provided data for this category; Serbia 3.99%, Croatia 0.52% and Estonia 0.05%. Typically, these students are educated in regular classes.

Figure 3.21 **Numbers of second language students by country as a percentage of all students in compulsory education and distribution by location**

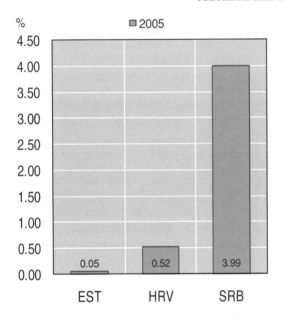
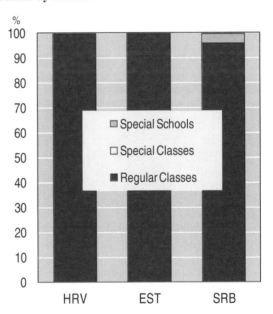

Disadvantaged students

Figure 3.22 shows the numbers of disadvantaged students by country, as a percentage of all students in compulsory education and where they are educated. Although only three countries provide data for this category, they indicate large variations in the proportions of students resourced. The range is from 3.22% in Croatia to 1.61% in Latvia and 0.09% in Bulgaria. The figure also shows that almost all disadvantaged students who receive additional resources follow the curriculum in regular classes, except in Bulgaria where 53.5% of them are placed in special schools.

Figure 3.22 **Numbers of disadvantaged students by country, as a percentage of all students in compulsory education**

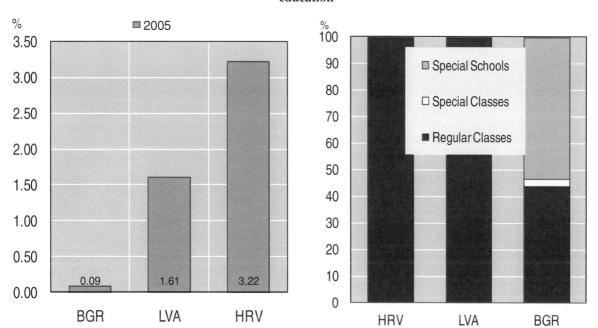

Conclusions

This chapter provided an analysis of available data based on the national categories used to provide additional resources for children and students who have difficulties accessing the curriculum as supplied by participating economies. It has looked at the proportions registered in educational statistics by category and by location of education. The data show substantial variation in categories used by countries and in the country prevalence rates over the period covering compulsory education. Furthermore, the location of education (regular schools, special classes, or special schools) can vary in a notable manner from country to country. For many categories at the extremes the education experiences of similar students would be very different in different economies. For instance, in one they might be educated in regular classes while in another they may be fully segregated from mainstream education.

Because of the different definitions in use of national categories for these students, the present study has adopted a simplified tripartite cross-national categorisation, referred to as A, B and C within the context of a resources model which has been outlined in previous chapters. The following chapters use this framework to describe the remainder of the data gathered by the quantitative part of the instrument.

References

OECD (2000), *Special Needs Education: Statistics and Indicators*, Paris, OECD.

OECD (2005), *Students with Disabilities, Learning Difficulties and Disadvantages: Statistics and Indicators*, Paris, OECD.

Chapter 4. Analysis of the Quantitative Data for Cross-National Categories A, B and C

In this chapter the data on individual national categories have been reclassified according to the tripartite taxonomy that broadly corresponds to students with disabilities, students with learning or behaviour difficulties and students with social disadvantages and has been subsequently analysed. Data on numbers of students and where they are educated is then presented on each of the cross-national categories in sequence, over the period of compulsory education. This is then followed by data on the non-compulsory phases of pre-primary and upper-secondary education.

Background

This chapter analyses the data provided by country experts in Tables 2, 3 and 4 of the Electronic Questionnaire and follows a similar format to that in the corresponding chapter in the publication *Students with Disabilities, Learning Difficulties and Disadvantages: Policies, Statistics and Indicators* (OECD, 2007).

As in OECD 2007, the data on individual national categories have been reclassified according to the three cross-national categories that correspond broadly to students with *disabilities* (A); students with learning or behaviour *difficulties* (B); and those with social *disadvantages* (C) (see Chapter 1 and the allocation matrix in Chapter 2). To avoid repetition of the term 'students within cross-national category', the terms disabilities, difficulties, and disadvantages are frequently used in this chapter as synonyms for the three cross-national categories.

The chapter is divided into sections covering each of the cross-national categories in sequence. Within each section, there is an initial discussion of data on students receiving additional resources over the period of compulsory education. This is followed data on the non-compulsory phases of pre-primary and upper secondary education where it is available.

In all figures, countries are ranked either in ascending order in terms of overall percentages or in descending order in terms of their distribution in regular classes. OECD means and medians are presented and refer to data for school-year 2005.

Availability of data

Table 4.1 illustrates the availability of data for the cross-national categories for eleven of the thirteen economies included in this study (the other two, Romania and Moldova were unable to provide data). Data are presented according to the location of education (special schools, special classes and regular classes) and levels or phases of education (compulsory education, pre-primary, primary, lower secondary and upper secondary).

It is clear that the amount of information which countries were able to provide varied widely from country to country. It is also clear that there are more sound and reliable data for students with disabilities than for those with learning difficulties or disadvantage. The most reliable data is to be found for students receiving additional resources over the period of compulsory education.

Table 4.1 also provides an indication of where future data collection should be expanded in individual countries in order to obtain eventually a full data set.

Table 4.1 **Availability of data for cross-national categories A, B and C, by location of education and level of education, 2005**

CATEGORY A

Special schools

Country	Compulsory education	Pre-primary education	Primary education	Lower secondary education	Upper secondary education
Bosnia and H.	✓	m	✓	✓	x
Bulgaria	✓	✓	✓	✓	✓
Croatia	✓	✓	✓	a	✓
Estonia	✓	m	✓	✓	✓
Kosovo	✓	✓	✓	✓	✓
Latvia	✓	m	✓	a	✓
Lithuania	✓	✓	✓	✓	✓
Malta	✓	x	✓	a	a
Montenegro	✓	✓	✓	a	✓
Serbia	✓	m	✓	✓	✓
Slovenia	✓	✓	✓	✓	✓

Special classes

Country	Compulsory education	Pre-primary education	Primary education	Lower secondary education	Upper secondary education
Bosnia and H.	x	x	x	x	x
Bulgaria	✓	✓	✓	✓	✓
Croatia	✓	✓	✓	a	✓
Estonia	✓	m	✓	✓	m
Kosovo	✓	m	✓	✓	m
Latvia	✓	m	✓	a	✓
Lithuania	✓	✓	✓	a	✓
Malta	✓	a	✓	a	a
Montenegro	✓	m	✓	a	a
Serbia	m	m	m	m	m
Slovenia	n	✓	n	n	n

Regular classes

Country	Compulsory education	Pre-primary education	Primary education	Lower secondary education	Upper secondary education
Bosnia and H.	x	x	x	x	x
Bulgaria	✓	✓	✓	✓	✓
Croatia	✓	✓	✓	a	✓
Estonia	✓	m	✓	✓	✓
Kosovo	m	m	m	m	m
Latvia	✓	m	✓	a	✓
Lithuania	✓	✓	✓	✓	✓
Malta	✓	✓	✓	✓	m
Montenegro	✓	✓	✓	a	✓
Serbia	✓	m	✓	m	m
Slovenia	✓	✓	✓	✓	✓

CATEGORY B

Special schools

Country	Compulsory education	Pre-primary education	Primary education	Lower secondary education	Upper secondary education
Bosnia and H.	✓	m	✓	✓	x
Bulgaria	✓	✓	✓	✓	✓
Croatia	✓	✓	✓	a	✓
Estonia	✓	m	✓	✓	n
Kosovo	a	a	a	a	a
Latvia	✓	m	✓	a	m
Lithuania	✓	✓	✓	✓	✓
Malta	✓	x	✓	a	a
Montenegro	✓	m	✓	a	✓
Serbia	a	a	a	a	a
Slovenia	✓	n	✓	✓	✓

Special classes

Country	Compulsory education	Pre-primary education	Primary education	Lower secondary education	Upper secondary education
Bosnia and H.	x	x	x	x	x
Bulgaria	✓	✓	✓	✓	✓
Croatia	✓	✓	✓	a	✓
Estonia	✓	m	✓	✓	m
Kosovo	a	a	a	a	a
Latvia	✓	m	✓	a	a
Lithuania	✓	✓	✓	a	✓
Malta	n	a	n	a	a
Montenegro	✓	m	✓	a	a
Serbia	m	m	m	m	m
Slovenia	n	✓	n	n	n

Regular classes

Country	Compulsory education	Pre-primary education	Primary education	Lower secondary education	Upper secondary education
Bosnia and H.	x	x	x	x	x
Bulgaria	✓	✓	✓	✓	✓
Croatia	✓	✓	✓	a	✓
Estonia	✓	m	✓	✓	m
Kosovo	m	m	m	m	m
Latvia	✓	m	✓	a	m
Lithuania	✓	✓	✓	✓	✓
Malta	✓	✓	✓	✓	m
Montenegro	✓	✓	✓	a	✓
Serbia	✓	m	✓	m	m
Slovenia	✓	✓	✓	✓	✓

CATEGORY C

Special schools

Country	Compulsory education	Pre-primary education	Primary education	Lower secondary education	Upper secondary education
Bosnia and H.	✓	m	✓	✓	x
Bulgaria	✓	n	✓	✓	✓
Croatia	a	a	a	a	a
Estonia	n	n	n	n	n
Kosovo	a	a	a	a	a
Latvia	a	a	a	a	a
Lithuania	✓	✓	✓	✓	a
Malta	a	a	a	a	a
Montenegro	✓	m	✓	a	✓
Serbia	✓	✓	✓	a	✓
Slovenia	a	a	a	a	a

Special classes

Country	Compulsory education	Pre-primary education	Primary education	Lower secondary education	Upper secondary education
Bosnia and H.	x	x	x	x	x
Bulgaria	✓	✓	✓	✓	✓
Croatia	a	a	a	a	a
Estonia	n	n	n	n	n
Kosovo	a	a	a	a	a
Latvia	a	a	a	a	a
Lithuania	✓	✓	✓	✓	a
Malta	a	a	a	a	a
Montenegro	✓	m	✓	a	a
Serbia	m	m	m	m	m
Slovenia	a	a	a	a	a

Regular classes

Country	Compulsory education	Pre-primary education	Primary education	Lower secondary education	Upper secondary education
Bosnia and H.	x	x	x	x	x
Bulgaria	✓	✓	✓	✓	✓
Croatia	✓	✓	✓	a	✓
Estonia	✓	m	✓	✓	✓
Kosovo	a	a	a	a	a
Latvia	✓	a	✓	a	✓
Lithuania	✓	✓	✓	✓	✓
Malta	a	a	a	a	a
Montenegro	✓	✓	✓	a	✓
Serbia	✓	m	✓	m	m
Slovenia	a	a	a	a	a

Symbols for missing data:

a - Data not applicable because the category does not apply.

m - Data missing, not available.

n - Magnitude is either negligible or zero.

x - Data included in another category/column of the table.

Data on cross-national category A (students receiving additional resources for disabilities)

Cross-national category A, as discussed in Chapter 1, roughly corresponds to needs arising from impairing conditions. All countries using categorical systems for special educational needs have national categories which they consider to fall within cross-national category A, although the number of such categories varies widely from country to country (see Table 2.2 in Chapter 2).

The period of compulsory education

Figure 4.1 shows the number of students with disabilities receiving additional resources within the period of compulsory education, as a percentage of all students in compulsory education. Although the period of compulsory education varies slightly from country to country (see Annex 2) all countries have national categories falling into the cross-national category A.

Countries vary substantially in the proportions of students with disabilities. Where full data are available the values range from 1.06% in Bulgaria to 4.31% in Lithuania – the median being 2.78% and the mean 2.53%. Five countries provide additional resources to more than 3.4% of students with disabilities: Serbia, Croatia, Estonia, Latvia and Lithuania. Slovenia is in line with the OECD median at 2.78% and Malta is slightly below it with 2.53%. On the other hand, Bulgaria, Montenegro and Bosnia and Herzegovina show a percentage only slightly above 1%.

Figure 4.1 **Numbers of students receiving additional resources over the period of compulsory education in cross-national category A as a percentage of all students in compulsory education, 2005**

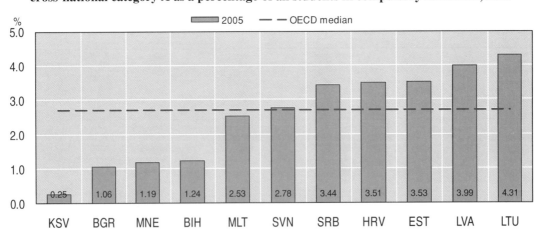

Note: Kosovo: data for regular classes are currently not readily available.

For OECD member countries the median is 2.72% and the mean is 2.58%. Further work would be needed at both national and international levels to understand these differences more fully and to determine whether some countries are unnecessarily over-identifying children while others may be under-identifying them.

Although there are still substantial variations between countries they are less marked than in the previous chapter for individual categories. Leaving Kosovo aside (as data for regular classes are currently not readily available), the ratio between the extremes is only of 1 to 4, in comparison, to 1 to 8 for some individual categories such as physical disabilities or intellectual disabilities. Comparing the data in terms of cross-national categories has the effect of smoothing the data.

The place of education

Figure 4.2 shows where students with disabilities are educated. Considering only the countries for which all data are available, they can be divided up in two groups corresponding to two different types of provision. In Malta, Serbia, Croatia, Montenegro, and Lithuania, the vast majority of these students are educated in regular classes (from 72% in Lithuania to 84% in Malta). On the other hand, 60% of students with disabilities are educated in special schools in Slovenia and between 70% and 95% are in special schools and special classes in Bulgaria, Estonia, and Latvia.

Figure 4.2 **Percentages of students receiving additional resources over the period of compulsory education in cross-national category A by location, 2005**

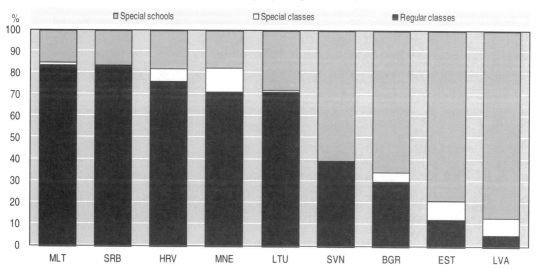

Note: Serbia: data on special classes are currently not readily available.

Pre-primary education

In OECD member countries, pre-primary education is regarded as especially important for children with disabilities and is reflected in an extension of free publicly provided education from age 0 onwards (OECD, 2007). Eight economies were able to provide data on the proportion of children in pre-primary education receiving additional resources for disabilities. Figure 4.3 shows that percentages within this group of economies vary from 0.84% in Bulgaria to 3.75% in Lithuania. The median number of children receiving additional resources for disabilities, as a percentage of all children in pre-primary education, is 1.13%, the mean is 1.67%. These figures are quite close to the OECD median and mean of 0.94% and 1.62% respectively.

Figure 4.3 **Numbers of students receiving additional resources in pre-primary education in cross-national category A as a percentage of all students in pre-primary education, 2005**

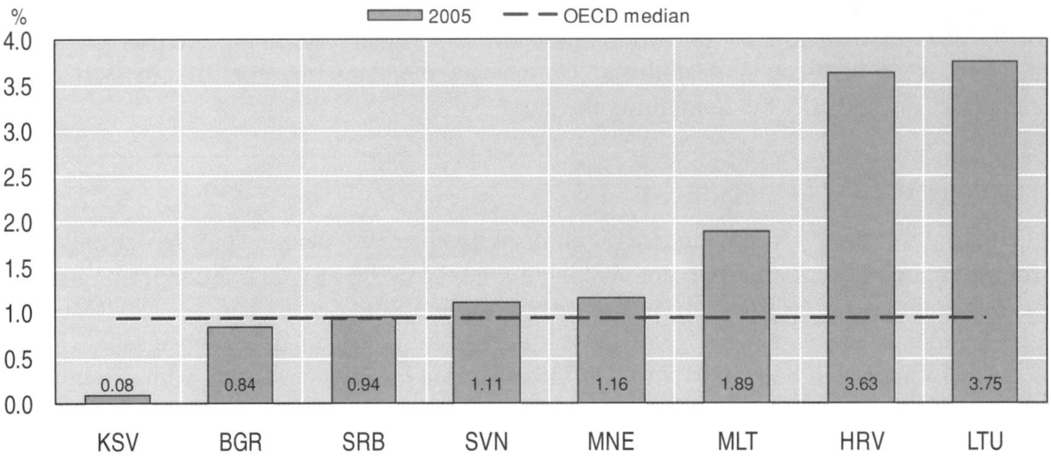

Note: Kosovo: data are available for special schools only.

The place of education

Figure 4.4 shows where these children are educated. It reveals that all such children are in segregated settings in Serbia but fully integrated in Malta. The remaining countries use a combination of special schools, special classes and regular classes.

Figure 4.4 **Percentages of students receiving additional resources in pre-primary education in cross-national category A by location, 2005**

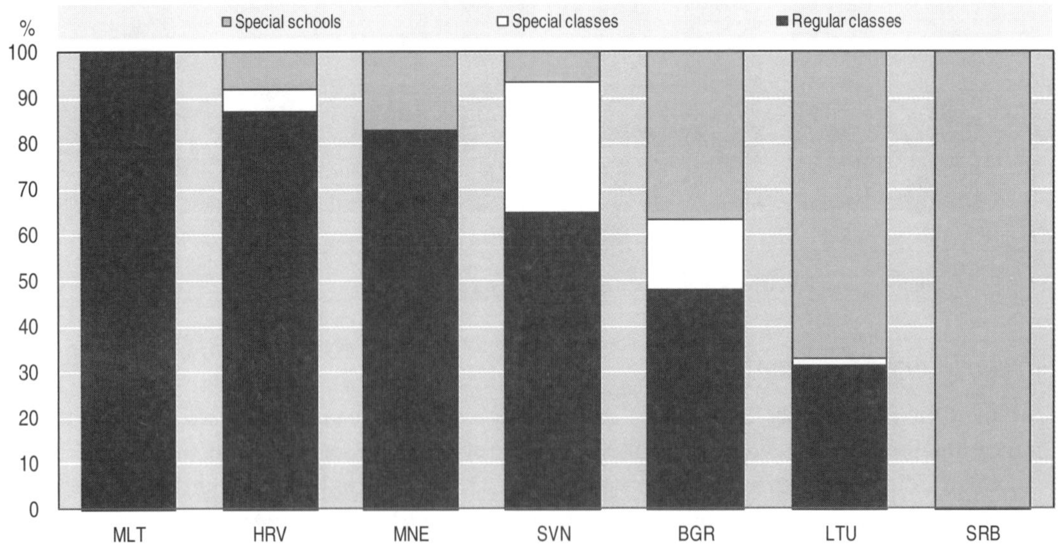

Note: Montenegro: data for special classes are not available.

Upper secondary education

Figure 4.5 shows the numbers of students with disabilities receiving additional resources in upper secondary education. Again it reveals substantial variation between countries providing full data with Latvia at 0.28% and Croatia at 3.69%. It is also evident that these figures are substantially lower than for those in the compulsory period (Figure 4.1).

Croatia, Latvia and Montenegro report an educational system that does not allow distinguishing lower secondary education from compulsory education. Typical age ranges for enrolment in upper secondary education for these countries are: Croatia from 14 to 19 years old; Latvia from 16 to 19; Montenegro from 14 to 18 years old.

The median number of students receiving additional resources for disabilities, for the ten economies reporting full data, as a percentage of all students in upper secondary education is 0.36% and the mean is 0.88%. These figures are substantially lower than the OECD median and mean which are 1.38% and 1.56% respectively.

Figure 4.5 **Numbers of students receiving additional resources in upper secondary education in cross-national category A as a percentage of all students in upper secondary education, 2005**

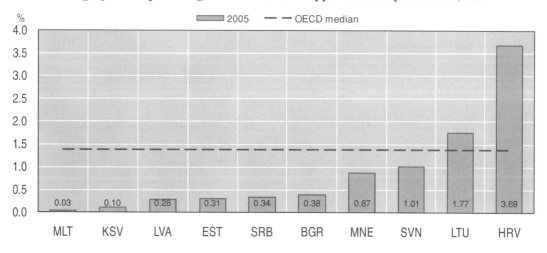

Notes: Kosovo: data are available for special schools only. Most likely there are students in special and regular classes but currently they cannot be quantified.
Malta: this percentage concerns students with intellectual disabilities only (category 1).
Serbia: data are available for special schools only. Data are not available for students in special and regular classes

The place of education

Figure 4.6 shows where students with disabilities are educated at the upper secondary level. The use of the two types of provision (segregation, inclusion) is evident. It emerges that the majority of these students are in segregated settings in Bulgaria, Estonia, and Latvia, and mostly integrated in Lithuania. Slovenia and Croatia integrate around 80% of them in regular classes. In Montenegro, students with disabilities in this phase of education are almost evenly distributed between special schools and regular classes.

Figure 4.6 **Percentages of students receiving additional resources in upper secondary education in cross-national category A by location, 2005**

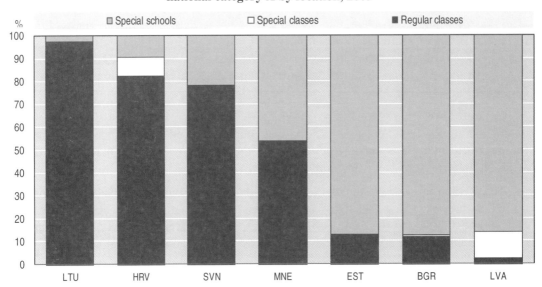

Note: Estonia: data are available for special schools. Data for regular classes are partially missing (category Intellectual disabilities).

Data on cross-national category B (students receiving additional resources for difficulties)

The quantity and quality of data relating to cross-national category B are inferior to that for cross-national category A (see Table 4.1). Cross-national category B, as discussed and defined in Chapter 1, refers to students with behavioural and emotional disorders, or specific difficulties in learning. The educational need is considered to arise primarily from problems in the interaction between the student and the educational context.

The period of compulsory education

Figure 4.7 shows the number of students with learning difficulties receiving additional resources within the period of compulsory education as a percentage of all students in compulsory education. All countries have categories falling into this broad category B. However, data for the categories making up category B are not available for Kosovo.

The figure below shows considerable variation across countries, ranging from 14.78% in Estonia to 0.21% in Bulgaria. The median is 2.37% and the mean is 3.80%. Lithuania also stands out with a high percentage of students in this category (9.08%). Then follow Serbia (4.35%), Croatia (3.19%), Latvia (2.50%) and Slovenia (2.23%). In Bosnia and Herzegovina, Bulgaria, Malta and Montenegro, the proportion of students with learning difficulties provided with additional resources is lower than 1% of the compulsory school age population.

The substantial variation in provision for students with difficulties in learning reflects the pattern of OECD member countries with Finland resourcing more than 23% of students, the UK more than 13% but at the other extreme with the Slovak Republic at 1%. Japan reports no students in category B. OECD median is 4.13% and OECD mean is 5.80%.

Figure 4.7 **Numbers of students receiving additional resources over the period of compulsory education in cross-national category B as a percentage of all students in compulsory education, 2005**

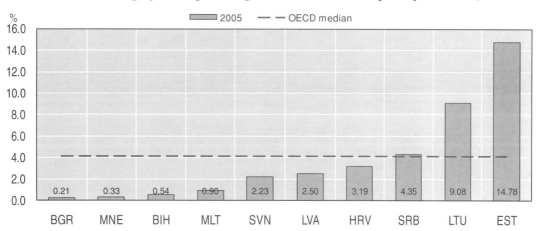

The place of education

Figure 4.8 shows the percentages of students with difficulties receiving additional resources over the period of compulsory education, by location. Compared with provisions for students with disabilities, there is much less variation between countries. Moreover, a pattern emerges: in all nine countries for which data are fully available, more than 70% of these students follow the curriculum in regular classes. This ranges from 72% in Bulgaria to 100% in Serbia. Three countries make some use of special classes: Bulgaria (6.8%), Estonia (7.1%) and Latvia (8.5%). The picture is slightly different from what is observed in OECD countries where a more substantial use of segregated provision is made in Belgium, in the Netherlands and in Germany (OECD, 2007).

Figure 4.8 **Percentages of students receiving additional resources over the period of compulsory education in cross-national category B by location, 2005**

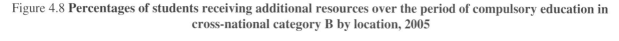

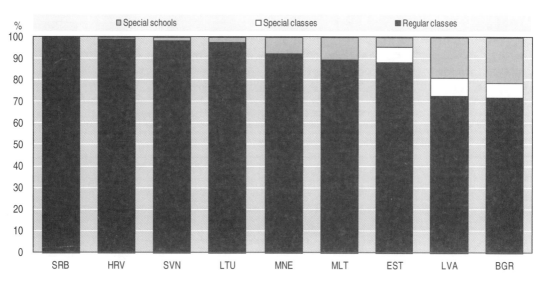

Note: Serbia: data on special classes are not available.

Pre-primary education

Figure 4.9 indicates the number of students with learning difficulties receiving additional resources in pre-primary/pre-school education, as a percentage of all students in pre-primary education. Six of the eleven economies in this study are able to provide data on this group of children and on where they are educated. In four countries, for which full data are available, the percentages of students receiving additional resources in this phase of education are quite low and vary between 0.1% and 0.2%. The only exceptions are Croatia (3.4%) and Lithuania (24.3%).

The median number of students receiving additional resources for difficulties, as a percentage of all students in pre-primary education is 0.20%; and the mean is 4.72%. The OECD median is 0.34% and the mean is 0.91%.

Figure 4.9 **Numbers of students receiving additional resources in pre-primary education in cross-national category B as a percentage of all students in pre-primary education, 2005**

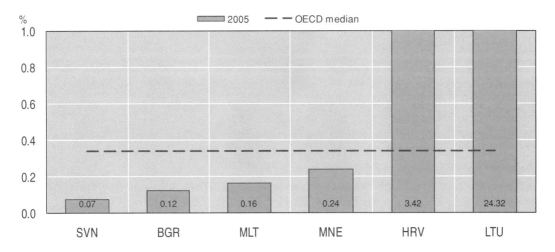

The place of education

Figure 4.10 shows where these children are educated – special schools, special classes or regular classes. The majority of countries include this group of children in regular schools or classes. However, Bulgaria (23.6%) and Croatia (5.2%) make some use of special schools. In Slovenia, 21.4% of students with learning difficulties are educated in special classes.

Figure 4.10 **Percentages of students receiving additional resources in pre-primary education in cross-national category B by location, 2005**

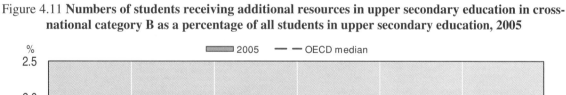

Notes: Malta: data for special schools and special classes are not applicable.

Montenegro: data for special schools and special classes are not currently available.

Upper secondary education

Figure 4.11 shows the number of students with learning difficulties receiving additional resources in upper secondary education, as a percentage of all students in upper secondary education. Six of the eleven economies in this study were able to provide data on this group of students and on where they are educated. In Bulgaria and in Estonia the percentages receiving additional resources in this phase of education are very low (0.03% and 0.10% respectively). Values are 0.37% in Montenegro and Slovenia, and 0.47% in Lithuania. Croatia (1.02%) indicates the highest percentage of students receiving additional resources in this phase of education.

Figure 4.11 **Numbers of students receiving additional resources in upper secondary education in cross-national category B as a percentage of all students in upper secondary education, 2005**

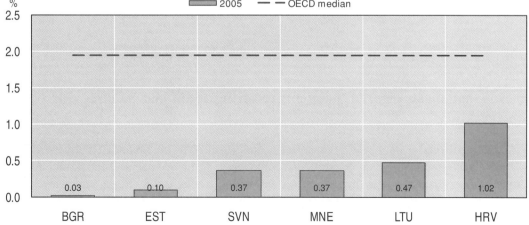

Note: Estonia: this percentage excludes students with temporary learning difficulties (category 12).

The median number of students receiving additional resources for difficulties, for the six countries reporting full data, as a percentage of all students in upper secondary education is 0.37%; and the mean is 0.39%. The OECD median, 1.95%, is notably higher and so is the mean, 3.53%.

The place of education

Figure 4.12 shows where students with difficulties receiving additional resources are educated at the upper secondary level. The use of the two types of provision (segregation, inclusion) is evident. It is clear that all such students are almost fully integrated in Lithuania, mostly included in regular settings in Slovenia and Croatia and the majority of them are in segregated settings in Bulgaria and Montenegro. In Estonia, these students would be educated most likely in regular schools but the information provided is currently partially missing.

These patterns are different from those in the corresponding section for OECD member countries where a more substantial use of inclusive provision is made (OECD, 2007).

Figure 4.12 **Percentages of students receiving additional resources in upper secondary education in cross-national category B by location, 2005**

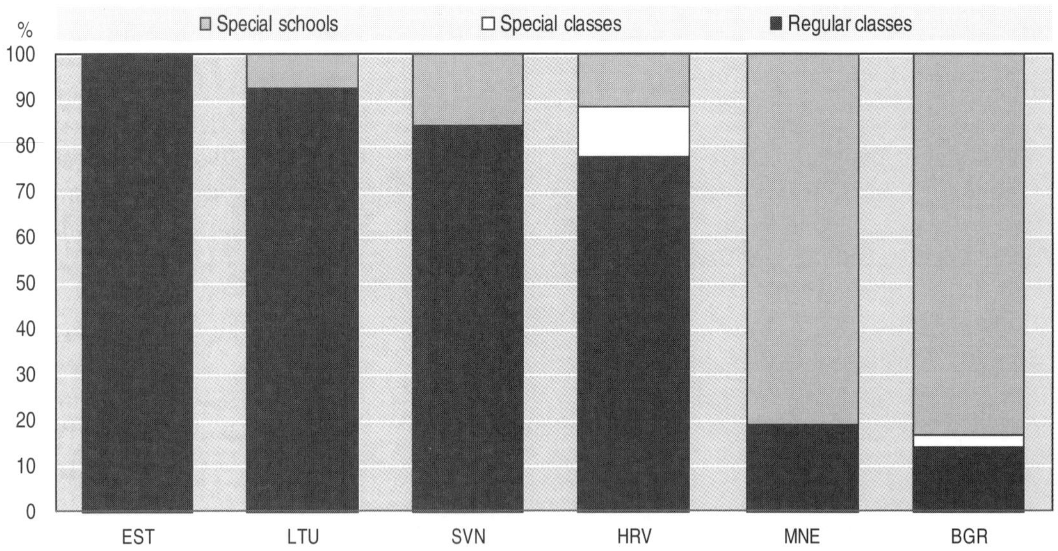

Note: Estonia: this percentage excludes students with temporary learning difficulties (category 12) who would most likely be placed in regular schools but the information provided is currently partially missing.

Data on cross-national category C (students receiving additional resources for disadvantages)

Cross-national category C, as defined and discussed in Chapter 1, covers those national categories referring to students considered to have special educational needs arising from disadvantages in their socio-economic background. Eight countries have categories falling into the broad category C. Kosovo, Malta and Slovenia do not have such categories (see Table 2.2).

Additional resources are particularly addressed to migrants or ethnic minorities mainly for language learning and preparation for compulsory schooling (preparatory classes before primary education). In some countries, these provisions fall under the definition of special education needs but in some others this is not the case.

The period of compulsory education

Figure 4.13 shows the number of students with disadvantages receiving additional resources within the period of compulsory education, as a percentage of all students in compulsory education.

The figures indicate that when categories of students with disadvantages are included in national systems, the numbers of students receiving additional resources are low. In fact, it is interesting to note that in contrast with the previous cross-national categories, the percentages presented here for category C are quite substantially lower than their equivalent in OECD countries (OECD, 2007). The median number of students receiving additional resources for disadvantages, for the eight economies reporting full data, as a percentage of all students in compulsory education is 0.68%. Given the variety of types of provision for students with disadvantages, the references to median or mean are to be taken with caution.

The difference between the extreme points is considerable. The percentages range from 0.02% in Bosnia and Herzegovina to 3.99% in Serbia. However, in the central part of the distribution, four countries (Estonia, Croatia, Montenegro, and Lithuania) show percentages between 0.4% and 1%, not too distant from the median.

Figure 4.13 **Numbers of students receiving additional resources over the period of compulsory education in cross-national category C as a percentage of all students in compulsory education, 2005**

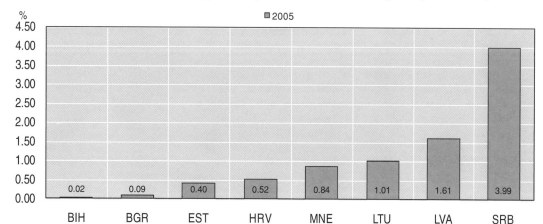

The place of education

Figure 4.14 shows the percentages of students with disadvantages receiving additional resources over the period of compulsory education, by location. The majority of countries providing data for the period of compulsory schooling educate students with disadvantages within compulsory education mostly in integrated settings. The pattern is very clear: in three of the seven countries for which data are available these students are all educated in regular classes (Croatia, Estonia and Latvia); and in Montenegro, Serbia and Lithuania the percentages range from 99% to 96%. On the other hand, data for Bulgaria depict a different picture, as the majority of students with disadvantages receiving additional resources are educated in segregated settings (53%) and special classes (3%) and approximately 44% are educated in regular classes.

With regard to the quality and quantity of data available on this group of students who are at risk because of disadvantage or their socio-economic background, it has to be stressed that these students are difficult to identify in the majority of countries. For countries which implement inclusive policies it is not always easy to identify separately additional resources allocated for the support of students with disadvantages but this does not of course mean that they do not identify and support this group of at-risk students.

Figure 4.14 **Percentages of students receiving additional resources over the period of compulsory education in cross-national category C by location, 2005**

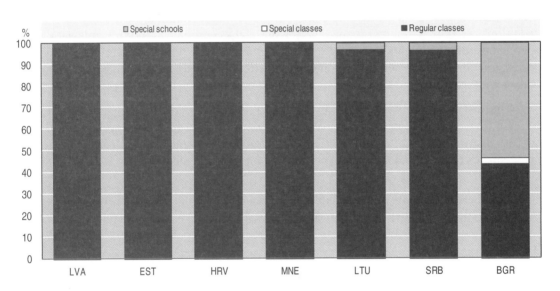

Notes: Latvia: data for special schools and special classes are not applicable.
Estonia: data for special schools and special classes are nil.
Croatia: data for special schools and special classes are not applicable.
Serbia: data for special classes are not available.

Pre-primary education

Figure 4.15 shows the number of students with disadvantages receiving additional resources in pre-primary education, as a percentage of all students in pre-primary education.

The figures below indicate that when categories of students with disadvantages are included in national systems, the numbers of students receiving additional resources are low. It is interesting to note that the percentages presented for category C are quite substantially lower than their equivalent in OECD member countries which vary considerably but can be quite high *e.g.* around 15% in Mexico and 12% in Belgium (Fr.) (OECD, 2007).

Figure 4.15 **Numbers of students receiving additional resources in pre-primary education in cross-national category C as a percentage of all students in pre-primary education, 2005**

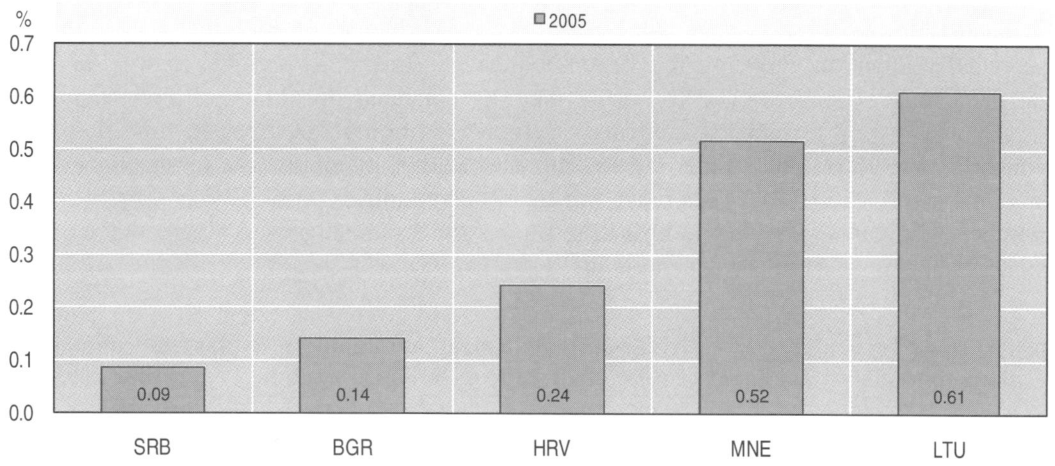

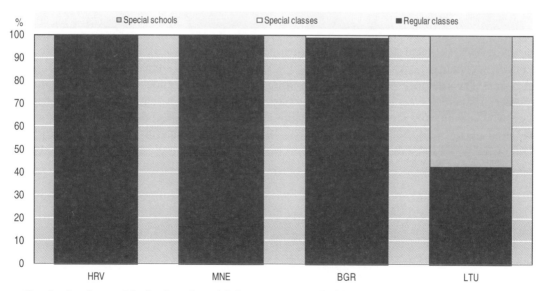

Note: Serbia: data for special and regular classes are currently not available.

The place of education

Figure 4.16 describes the distribution of disadvantaged children receiving additional resources in pre-primary education in special schools, special classes and regular classes. Two of the four countries providing data, Croatia and Montenegro, educate all students with disadvantages in inclusive settings. Notable exception is Lithuania where there is a combination of provision in both segregated and inclusive settings although the majority are educated in special schools. In Bulgaria, the majority of students with disadvantages are educated in regular classes and 1.2% in special classes.

Figure 4.16 **Percentages of students receiving additional resources in pre-primary education in cross-national category C by location, 2005**

Notes: Croatia: data for special schools and special classes are not applicable.
Montenegro: data for special schools and special classes are not applicable.
Lithuania: data for special classes are not applicable.

Upper secondary education

Figure 4.17 shows the number of disadvantaged students receiving additional resources in upper secondary education, as a percentage of all students in upper secondary education. Seven of the eleven countries in this study are able to provide data on this group of students and on where they are educated. In almost all countries, the percentages of disadvantaged students receiving additional resources in this phase of education are very small (under 0.2%). Bulgaria (0.05%) supports the least numbers of students and Latvia (0.85%) the most. For the seven countries presented here, the median number of students receiving additional resources for disadvantages as a percentage of all students in upper secondary education is 0.11%.

Figure 4.17 **Numbers of students receiving additional resources in upper secondary education in cross-national category C as a percentage of all students in upper secondary education, 2005**

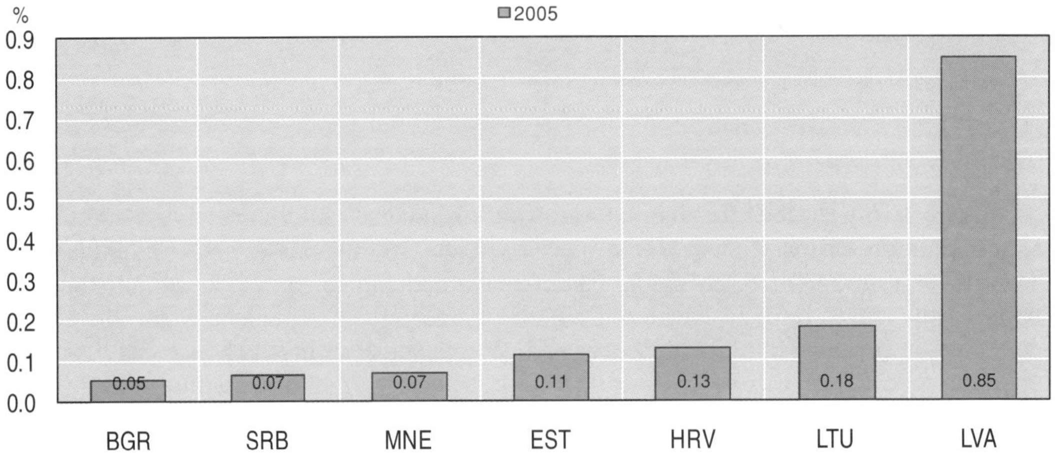

Note: Serbia: data for special and regular classes are currently not available.

The place of education

Figure 4.18 illustrates where disadvantaged children receiving additional resources in upper secondary education are educated – special schools, special classes and regular classes. The majority of countries providing data educate students with disadvantages mostly in inclusive settings. A notable exception is Bulgaria, where the majority of these students are in segregated settings. In Montenegro, 91% of disadvantaged students are in regular classes and 9% are educated in special schools. These patterns are comparable to those for OECD member countries where a very substantial use of inclusive provision is made (OECD, 2007).

Figure 4.18 **Percentages of students receiving additional resources in upper secondary education in cross-national category C by location, 2005**

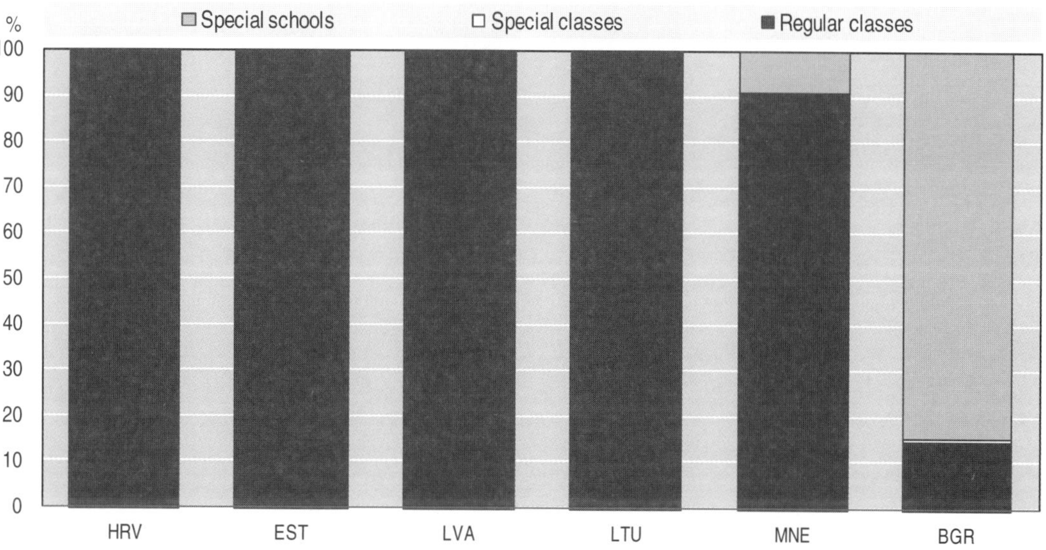

Notes: Croatia: data for special schools and special classes are not applicable.
Montenegro: data for special classes are not applicable.
Estonia: data for special schools and special classes are nil.
Latvia: data for special schools and special classes are not applicable.
Lithuania: data for special schools and special classes are not applicable.

Comparisons between cross-national categories, in compulsory education and upper secondary education

Table 4.2 and Figure 4.19 provide comparison data restricted to the six countries for which data are available for students in cross-national categories A and B. Data are presented for the phases of compulsory education and upper secondary education. For category A, the means are 2.39% in compulsory education and 1.40% in upper secondary education. These mean percentages of students drop by 41% from compulsory education to upper secondary education. This is comparable with what happens in OECD countries. For category B, the means drop by 84% between compulsory education and upper secondary level, from 2.62% to 0.42%. This represents a much more significant change, in comparison to the equivalent percentage for OECD countries where the mean decreases by only 39%.

These data reveal that on average countries' educational provision during the compulsory phase of education is similar to that of OECD countries while in upper secondary education there is a clear drop in provision. For category A the change is rather similar but for category B it is very much larger. The smaller proportion of students staying on to upper secondary education is of itself not surprising since many of these students would leave school anyway at the end of the compulsory period. In five of the six countries providing data, the reduction in the numbers of students staying on is very substantial – the exception is Montenegro where the proportion increases – suggesting that there is considerable work to be done to help to keep more of these children in upper secondary education which would open the way for tertiary education hence tackling poverty and social exclusion.

Table 4.2 **Percentages of students receiving additional resources in compulsory and in upper secondary education in cross-national categories A and B**

Cross-national category A				Cross-national category B			
	Compulsory education	Upper secondary education	Difference		Compulsory education	Upper secondary education	Difference
Bosnia	1.48	0.68	-54%	Bosnia	0.66	0.26	-61%
Bulgaria	1.06	0.38	-64%	Bulgaria	0.21	0.03	-88%
Croatia	3.51	3.69	5%	Croatia	3.19	1.02	-68%
Lithuania	4.31	1.77	-59%	Lithuania	9.08	0.47	-95%
Montenegro	1.19	0.87	-27%	Montenegro	0.33	0.37	11%
Slovenia	2.78	1.01	-64%	Slovenia	2.23	0.37	-84%
Mean	2.39	1.40	-41%	Mean	2.62	0.42	-84%
Median	2.13	0.94	-56%	Median	1.44	0.37	-74%
OECD mean	2.84	1.65	-42%	OECD mean	5.80	3.53	-39%
OECD median	2.85	1.58	-44%	OECD median	4.13	1.95	-53%

Figure 4.19 **Percentages of students receiving additional resources in compulsory and in upper secondary education in cross-national categories A and B - means**

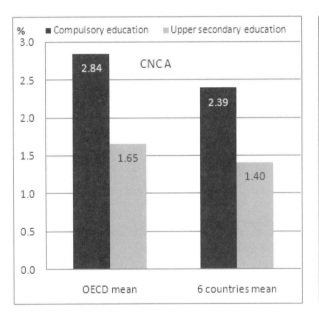
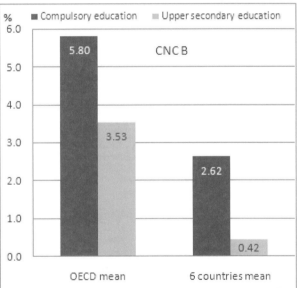

Discussion and conclusions

This chapter uses the OECD resource-based definition of special education to identify students who are receiving additional resources in order to access the curriculum and then breaks this large group down into the three sub-groups of those with disabilities, learning difficulties and disadvantages. This approach helps to reduce problems arising from different national definitions and concepts of special needs that exist across participating economies (see Table 2.2). Thus grouping special needs students into three general categories has the effect of smoothing the data and overcoming problems related to classification errors. However, the data presented in this chapter show substantial differences among economies *vis-à-vis* the numbers of students with disabilities, learning difficulties and disadvantages that, nevertheless, are smaller than those found when comparing individual national categories.

As far as the place of education is concerned, participating economies make use of special schools, special classes and regular classes. In addition there is substantial pre-school provision which is essential to give these children the skills and behaviour necessary to benefit as fully as possible from regular educational provision. Early identification and intervention for children who have difficulties with access to the curriculum is essential. Research shows (EC, 2008) that participation in free, high quality pre-primary education can have long-lasting benefits for achievement and socialisation during an individual's schooling and later career development because it can facilitate later learning.

There is less evidence for the extensive provision of upper secondary education for SENDDD students. The reasons for this need further research but it is clear that a lack of upper secondary provision clearly hampers students with disabilities, learning difficulties and disadvantages from developing their full educational potential and inhibits access to higher education.

The data presented in this chapter show substantial differences among countries *vis-à-vis* the numbers of students with disabilities, learning difficulties and disadvantages receiving additional resources to make progress with the curriculum. These differences are however smaller than those found when comparing individual national categories in the previous chapter.

There is also considerable variation among countries in the use of educational settings where students are educated (*i.e.* segregated versus inclusive).

Students with disabilities

Provision for students with disabilities shows similar patterns to OECD member countries both in terms of levels of resourcing and educational settings.

In most economies, there are higher percentages of students receiving additional resources for disabilities in compulsory education than in pre-primary and upper secondary education.

There is substantial variation in the proportions of students receiving additional resources for disability among countries. It is unclear what underlies these differences. In addition to variations in the proportion of students with disabilities, there are national differences in the conceptualisation of disability, identification procedures, educational practices, comprehensiveness of provision, and policy priorities.

Students with learning difficulties

Provision for students with learning difficulties shows a pattern slightly below that of OECD countries for the numbers of students provided with extra resources, and illustrates a more uniform distribution regarding the placement of students in special schools, special classes and regular classes.

In most economies, there are higher percentages of students receiving additional resources for learning difficulties in compulsory education than in pre-primary and upper secondary education. It is clear that these students are harder to identify before entering compulsory education.

Students with disadvantages

Findings and issues concerning students receiving additional resources for disadvantages (cross-national category C) mirror those described for students with disabilities and difficulties. In fact, countries vary *vis-à-vis* identification procedures, educational practices, comprehensiveness of provision, and policy priorities.

Provision for students with disadvantages shows a pattern clearly below that of OECD member countries. The numbers of students identified as receiving additional resources are extremely low in this group of economies. Further discussions will help in understanding who these students are.

Percentages in the educational settings show a similar distribution as OECD countries which privileges inclusive provisions in most countries. However, a few economies still make use of segregated settings for the education of this group of students.

In most countries, there are higher percentages of students receiving additional resources for disadvantages in compulsory education than in pre-primary and upper secondary education.

General comments

The educational setting in which students with disabilities receive additional resources is of particular policy interest. In some economies these students are educated in special schools while in others they may be in special classes or regular classes. Such differences reveal potential inequities in provision in countries and will give students very different educational and socialising experiences. Equity considerations lead to the position that, wherever possible, students with disabilities difficulties and disadvantages are educated in regular, mainstream schools rather than in separate institutions. In fact, the educational and social experiences of special schools and regular schools are different, and this could be inequitable in terms of students' access to post-compulsory education and the labour market.

The different national policies concerning inclusion provide an explanation for these differences; these policies may be influenced by features of regular schools and their curriculum, and the training and attitudes of teacher that may facilitate or obstruct inclusion practices. Furthermore, there may be features of special schools that are viewed by parents and educators as desirable. Also, different cultural and societal views may influence this choice.

Recent studies (*e.g.* OECD, 1999) reveal that to make inclusive education work evidence points towards a need to allow schools to become learning organisations through a process of adaptation to a more diverse set of student needs, including students with severe disabilities. This will result in flexible provision that can provide additional support to all students in the school. Evidence has shown how non-disabled students also benefit from this extra support.

Overall, countries which make extensive use of special schooling need to continually monitor how children come to be referred to them as well as the nature and consequences of the provision in such schools. In addition to this, countries that place a strong emphasis on inclusive education in regular schools need an on-going assessment process to ensure that its objectives are being achieved.

References

OECD (1999), *Inclusive Education at Work, Students with Disabilities in Mainstream Schools*, Paris, OECD.

OECD (2005), *Students with Disabilities, Learning Difficulties and Disadvantages: Statistics and Indicators*, Paris, OECD.

OECD (2007), *Students with Disabilities, Learning Difficulties and Disadvantages: Policies, Statistics and Indicators*, Paris, OECD.

European Commission (2008), Progress Report towards the Lisbon Objectives in Education and Training, Indicators and Benchmarks, EC.

Chapter 5. Analysis of the Quantitative Data – Age and Gender

This chapter provides additional descriptive information on all students with disabilities, learning difficulties and disadvantages enrolled in educational programmes in special schools, special classes and regular classes classified by age and gender. It also discusses the preponderance of numbers of boys over girls in a wide range of analyses (educational setting, cross-national category, age of student, or phase of education).

Background

The first part of this chapter provides an analysis of the data on age and gender based on Table 6 of the Electronic Questionnaire. Table 6 asks for information on all students with disabilities, learning difficulties and disadvantages enrolled in educational programmes in special schools, special classes and regular classes classified by age and gender. Table 6 also asks for information on students not registered in the education system.

The second part of the chapter provides further analysis of the data collected in Tables 2, 3 and 4 of the Instrument based on gender breakdowns and by cross-national category. Data from Tables 2, 3 and 4 have formed the content of previous chapters.

Data by age, gender and location

Nine of the eleven economies presenting data for 2005 were able to provide breakdowns by age for students with special education needs. All nine provided data on special schools, eight on special classes and on regular classes.

Figures 5.1, 5.2 and 5.3 show the age distributions in special schools, special classes and regular classes respectively. These figures also show gender breakdowns, where gender data are available, and the overall sum of males and females.

Cohort size has been taken into account so the figures presented here are percentages of students in each age group. Data are presented following the format of Table 6 in the Electronic Questionnaire which asked for age breakdowns that range from years <3 to 19.

Close inspection between Table 6 and Tables 2, 3 and 4 reveal some inconsistencies. A few economies provided data by age which was not exhaustive of the whole population concerned. It is also worth noting that there are unknown numbers of children with disabilities, learning difficulties and disadvantages who are out of the school system. This phenomenon varies considerably from country to country. The percentages in this chapter are based on students in school only. Therefore, the following analyses must bear this point in mind.

Special schools

Figure 5.1 shows the numbers of students receiving additional resources in special schools by age and gender from ages <3 to 19. It reveals more availability of data for students receiving additional resources in the age range from 5-19. Most economies show an increase in the proportion of students in special schools from ages 5-6 up to about age 15. This is the case for Bulgaria, Estonia, Latvia, and Serbia. In Lithuania the overall trend is similar but it is less smooth. Croatia is a notable exception as the numbers of students in special schools are steadily increasing during the whole schooling period. Kosovo, Malta and Montenegro also show somewhat different patterns, but this may be because the numbers of students concerned are very low.

Economies in the figures below also show that there is a preponderance of males over females at most ages except in Bulgaria where data are not available. This result will be discussed in more detail later in this chapter in the section on gender.

Figure 5.1 **Percentages of students receiving additional resources in special schools by age and gender (2005)**

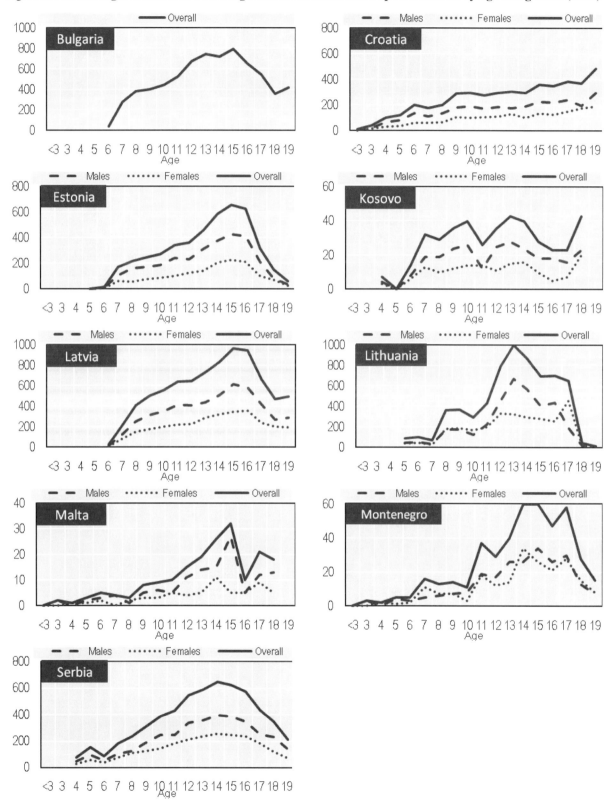

Special classes

Figure 5.2 shows the numbers of students in special classes by age and gender from ages <3 to 19. It reveals more availability of data for students receiving additional resources in the age range from 5/6 to 19. There is little data available below 5 years of age. Only Croatia, Lithuania and Malta show age breakdowns below primary education age. Kosovo and Montenegro provide data from ages 7 to 15.

The extent to which countries make use of special classes varies greatly. Only Croatia, Estonia, and Latvia show a wider use of special classes.

The pattern for special classes is more difficult to categorise than for special schools. Broadly speaking, there is a tendency for lower numbers to be found at both the youngest and oldest age ranges as it is shown in special schools as well. There are two patterns. The first shows a steady increase in the numbers attending special classes (Croatia, and Estonia). These two countries make use of special classes mostly at the secondary level. The second pattern shows a tendency for an increase in numbers up to a peak at ages 9-12 (Bulgaria, Kosovo, Latvia, Lithuania and Montenegro). With the exception for Bulgaria, the decrease after the peak is rather rapid. This may reflect change in school organisation between primary and secondary schools. Malta, on the other hand, shows a rather different picture across the age range but the overall numbers of students concerned are too low to be fully analysed. Croatia and Estonia make use of special classes mostly at the secondary level.

Figure 5.2 again illustrates the higher preponderance of males than females across the age range. Lithuania is a notable exception and this outcome calls for further explanation. Bulgaria provides no age breakdown data for special classes.

Figure 5.2 **Percentages of students receiving additional resources in special classes by age and gender**

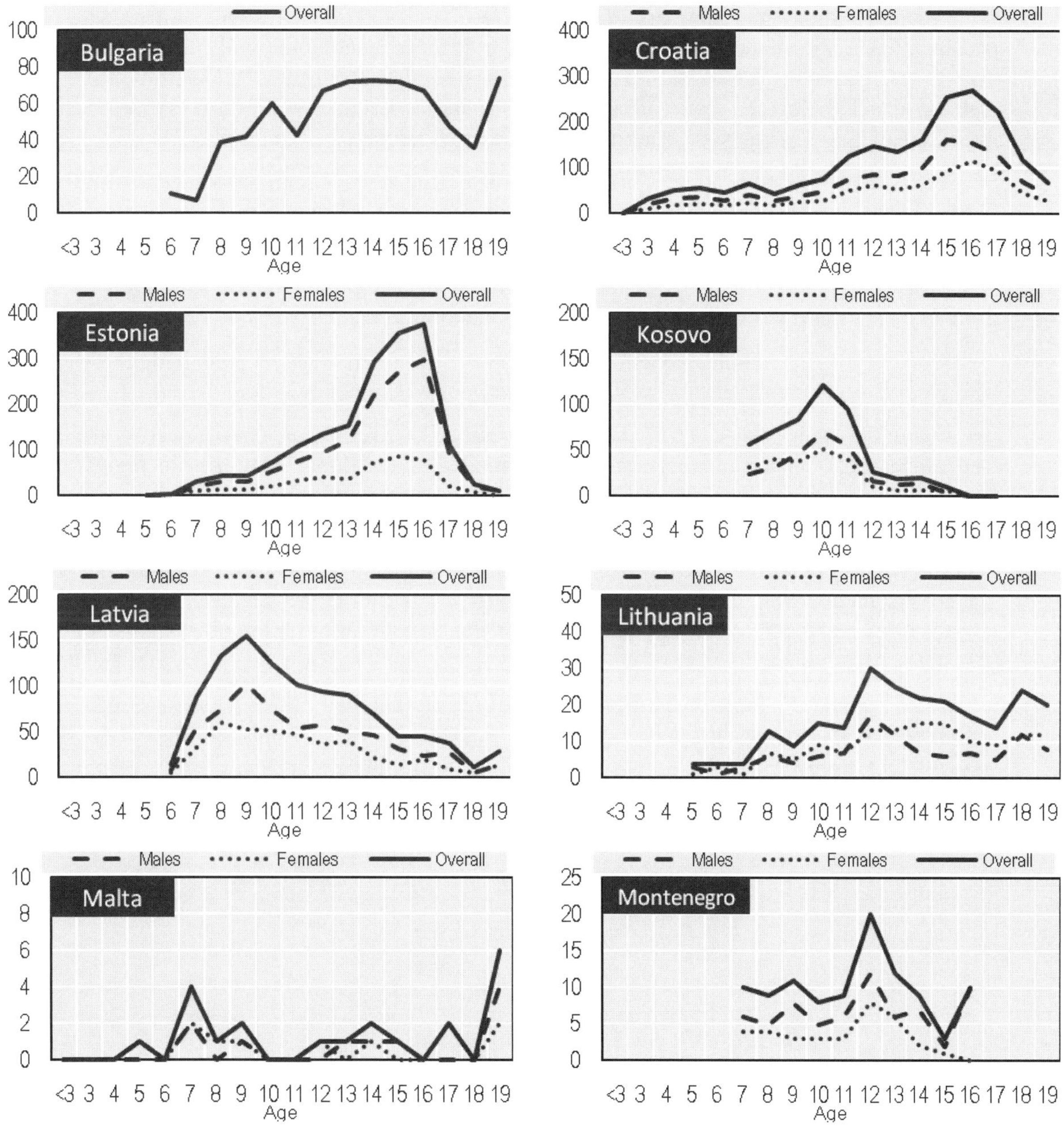

Regular classes

Figure 5.3 shows the numbers of students receiving additional resources in regular classes by age and gender from ages <3 to 19. It again reveals more availability of data for students receiving additional resources in the age range from 6 to 19. There is little data available below 6 years of age. Only Bulgaria, Croatia and Malta show age breakdowns below primary education age. Serbia provides data from ages 6 to 14.

Two patterns emerge here. Bulgaria, Estonia, Lithuania, Malta, Montenegro and Serbia show a peak in numbers during primary education followed by a fairly steady decline, except in Serbia at age 11 where there is a second peak.

Croatia and Latvia show a different pattern, with a regular increase until age 15 followed by a sharp decrease in the last years of schooling.

Montenegro is a notable exception as the percentages of students receiving additional resources in regular classes are steadily decreasing during the whole school period.

Figure 5.3 again shows the higher preponderance of males than females across the age range. Data on the numbers of students receiving additional resources in regular classes by age and gender is less sparse for the group of economies described below than for OECD countries (OECD, 2007).

Although more of these economies than OECD countries (OECD, 2007) can provide data on students with disabilities, learning difficulties and disadvantages in regular classes it has to be noted that no country was able to provide information on students not registered in the education system.

Some economies were able to provide data on the number of boys and girls over different age ranges as shown in Figures 5.1, 5.2 and 5.3. These data are aggregated across cross-national categories A, B and C. In order to analyse gender data by cross-national categories, another set of data was used in the next section and it refers to the period of compulsory schooling.

Figure 5.3 **Percentages of students receiving additional resources in regular classes by age and gender**

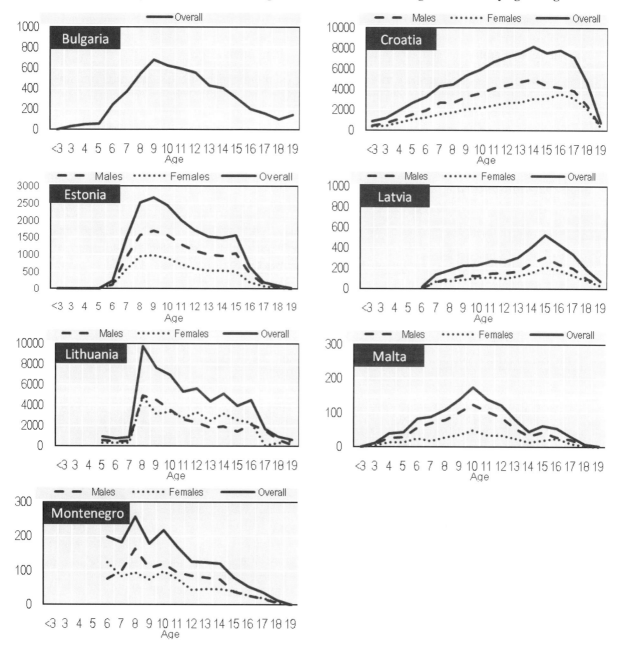

Data by gender and cross-national category

As highlighted in the previous section, a consistent finding reported in previous OECD work on the educational provision for students with disabilities, learning difficulties and disadvantages was the preponderance of numbers of boys over girls in a wide range of analyses (educational setting, cross-national or national category, age of student, or phase of education, etc.) This split was typically around 60% boys and 40% girls with disabilities and closer to 50/50 *vis-à-vis* students with disadvantages. However, the proportions concerning students with difficulties were even greater, *e.g.* 70% boys and 30% girls (OECD, 2007).

These findings are fully replicated in this study. Particularly, there are approximately 60% of boys in category A, 65% in category B and between 50% and 60% in category C. The section at the end of the chapter will explain them more fully.

The previous section showed that the higher preponderance of boys than girls remains strongly in evidence in the age breakdown data in special schools, special classes and regular classes in most economies. In the following analysis the data are derived from Tables 2, 3 and 4 and covers the period of compulsory education only. The data are broken down by gender and by cross-national categories A, B and C.

Cross-national category A

Figure 5.4 shows the distribution of boys and girls receiving additional resources for disabilities during the period of compulsory education. The mean for the ten economies presented in the figure is 59.6%. Boys outnumber girls in all economies with a ratio of approximately 3:2. Only Lithuania stands outside the range of 55-65%.

Figure 5.4 **Percentages of boys over the period of compulsory education in cross-national category A (2005)**

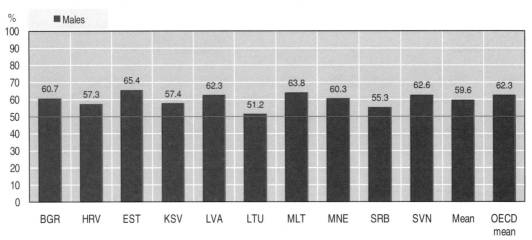

Note: Slovenia: data include special schools only because gender breakdowns are not available for special classes and regular classes.

Cross-national category B

Figure 5.5 shows the distribution of boys and girls receiving additional resources for difficulties during the period of compulsory education. Boys outnumber girls in all countries with a higher ratio than for students with disabilities as shown in Figure 5.4. The mean for the eight countries presented in Figure 5.5 is 64.6%. Again, Lithuania is a notable exception. There is a significant difference between the scores for students with disabilities and students with difficulties.

Figure 5.5 **Percentages of boys over the period of compulsory education in cross-national category B**

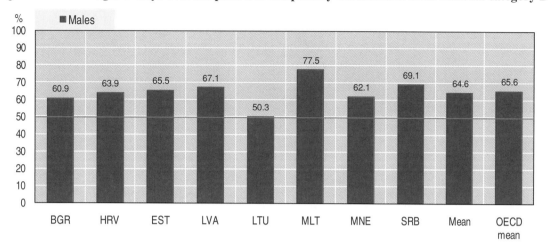

Cross-national category C

Figure 5.6 shows the distribution of boys and girls receiving additional resources for disadvantages during the period of compulsory education. The mean for the seven countries presented in the figure is 54.9%. Boys outnumber girls in almost all countries except Lithuania where the situation is reversed. Inspection of the data shows a ratio closer to 50% than for students receiving additional resources for disabilities and difficulties. This trend is in line with OECD data (mean = 55.3%).

Figure 5.6 **Percentages of boys over the period of compulsory education in cross-national category C**

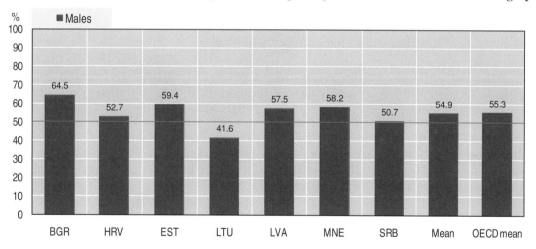

Table 5.1 shows the mean distribution of boys receiving additional resources for disabilities, learning difficulties and disadvantages during the period of compulsory education. Percentages for disabilities cluster closely around the 60/40 boy/girl mean; percentages for students with learning difficulties are more variable but the mean ratio is near two boys for one girl, which also corresponds to the OECD mean. Finally, percentages for students with disadvantages are typically lower than the previous ones. These patterns are in line with OECD means.

Table 5.1 **Percentages of boys over the period of compulsory education, by cross-national category**

Percentage of males	Cross-national category		
	A	B	C
Mean	59.6	64.6	54.9
OECD mean	62.3	65.6	55.3

Summary

With only an isolated exception there are more boys than girls receiving additional resources in all three cross-national categories during the period of compulsory education. The notable exception is represented by Lithuania.

A number of possible reasons have been identified by the OECD study to account for the relative numbers of boys receiving more additional resources than girls, including factors such as biology and behaviour, and each may play some role (for a fuller discussion see OECD, 2007). These include evidence that:

- boys seem more prone than girls to illness and trauma and therefore might require extra resources in their schooling;

- in some societies the education of males is given greater social priority than that of females and hence greater support;

- males adopt more noticeably deviant behaviours than females thus becoming identified and labelled;

- schooling is becoming increasingly "feminised".

Since the observed superfluity of boys have substantial implications for equity of any educational system further work is needed to understand these differences that should focus on outcomes linked to the impact of the additional resources that are invested.

The gender differences in provision for students with disabilities are sufficiently marked for this to be a priority focus. This is particularly clear when countries examine the basis by which students are identified for different educational programmes, and the long-term consequences of participation in those programmes.

Conclusion

The chapter provided additional descriptive information on all students with disabilities, learning difficulties and disadvantages enrolled in educational programmes in special schools, special classes and regular classes classified by age and gender.

It confirmed that there is generally higher quality data concerning students in special school programmes. It also revealed more availability of data on special classes and regular classes. This contrasts with OECD countries where few of them were able to provide adequate data on these two settings.

It further substantiated the consistent findings concerning the preponderance of numbers of males over females in a wide range of analyses carried out in OECD and OAS countries (OECD, 2007; OECD, 2007a). There are usually more male students receiving additional resources than females, regardless of whether data are analysed by educational setting, cross-national or national category, age of student, or phase of education.

References

OECD (2007), *Students with Disabilities, Learning Difficulties and Disadvantages: Policies, Statistics and Indicators*, Paris, OECD.

OECD (2007a), *Students with Disabilities, Difficulties and Disadvantages: Statistics and Indicators of OAS countries*, OECD/Edebe, Paris.

Chapter 6. Synthesis of Country Reports on Statistics and Indicators[6]

> *This chapter looks more closely at the processes leading to data collection and synthesizes the statistics and indicators regarding students with special education needs and those at risk in South Eastern Europe, Malta and the Baltic States based on data provided by three sets of country reports. It provides recommendations for improving data collection and quality efforts so that important questions about participation in education for different groups of students may be answered.*

Introduction

This chapter is a synthesis report on statistics and indicators of students with special education needs and those at risk in South Eastern Europe (SEE), Malta and the Baltic States. It is based on the information and data provided by three sets of country reports:

- Final reports of the micro projects on statistics and data gathering (eight South Eastern European economies, OECD, 2007).

- Country reports based on the situation of data gathering in nine South Eastern European economies, three Baltic countries and Malta, as produced in the joint OECD/CRELL study.

- Statistical data and background information as provided in the OECD publication *Education Policies for Students at Risk and Those with Disabilities in South Eastern Europe* (OECD, 2006) and the findings from the Follow-Up Visits October 2006-January 2007 [OECD, EDU/EDPC(2007)21].

A draft synthesis report was presented to country representatives in June 2008 at the joint CRELL/OECD meeting on Indicators on the Educational Provision for Students with Disabilities, learning Difficulties and Disadvantages held in Tallinn, Estonia. Clarifications and amendments were made to the final report as a result of written comments provided by country experts.

The purpose of the chapter is to provide an analysis of the status of data collection procedures and processes in each country, identify areas that need further clarification and future development, and to provide recommendations for a programme of work to improve data collection efforts and to collect data that can be convertible for use by international organisations such as *e.g.* OECD, European Commission, UNESCO, and World Bank.

---

[6] This chapter was edited by Lani Florian, Martyn Rouse and Maida Becirevic with Peter Evans, Marcella Deluca and Gerhard Kowar.

The region of South East Europe consists of: Albania, Bosnia and Herzegovina, Bulgaria, Croatia, Romania, Serbia, Montenegro, and the Former Yugoslav Republic of Macedonia (FYRoM). This chapter adds Slovenia and Moldova to this list. Albania and FYRoM are not covered. The status within Europe of the nine South Eastern European economies included in this report, the three Baltic countries and Malta is varied. Seven states have membership of the European Union: Estonia, Latvia, Lithuania, Slovenia and Malta joined in 2004, Romania and Bulgaria in 2007; Croatia is currently negotiating membership; Bosnia and Herzegovina, Montenegro, Serbia and Kosovo are considered potential candidates; and Moldova is considered a future enlargement possibility. Malta is also a member of the Commonwealth of Nations, having gained independence from Britain in 1964.

Summary

This chapter is structured around the guiding questions each country was asked to answer about the current national context. These questions were organised under three headings which form three of the sections of this chapter: (1) identification, (2) data flow, and (3) monitoring. Summary tables were produced for each guiding question enabling the identification of areas that need further clarification and future development. A final section identifies key areas for action arising from the analysis of the current situation and provides recommendations for a programme of work to improve data collection and quality.

All of the economies covered in this review have adopted human rights conventions and are making significant efforts to improve data collection and monitoring procedures for producing statistics and indicators for students with disabilities, learning difficulties and disadvantages (SENDDD). Progress towards producing reliable statistics varies between economies as can be seen from the tabulation of the country replies for each of the guiding questions. These tabulations also show the range of replies to some questions and an absence of replies to others. This suggests differences in how those producing the reports interpreted the guiding questions. Lack of infrastructure is also a key difficulty for many of these economies. Progress in developing a valid and reliable infrastructure will depend on establishing clarity of purpose and a continuing discussion about terminology and categories for data collection.

As in other economies, data on disability are often collected for health, education and social welfare benefit decisions. However, in economies that are not yet able to register all births, or provide much in the way of benefits, there are problems in determining incidence of disability even when prevalence is stable, because of the phenomenon of 'missing or invisible' children. This creates particular challenges for the development of reliable data systems. Supporting the development of infrastructure for data collection and monitoring is a key area for future development with actions needed to support a programme of work on conceptual, technical and legal levels. Continuing professional development for key staff will be an important element of this task.

Current systems for data collection reflect different national contexts and policy concerns which are, to varying degrees, of relevance to educational concerns. While the OECD's three cross-national categories represent an important advance in generating data that can be used for comparative purposes, barriers to the establishment of systems and procedures that will enable them to generate reliable and valid data remain salient in many (but not all) countries. On-going technical assistance will be needed to support these economies in the development of data systems that can generate data convertible for use international organisations.

While policy development and data collection activities have been supported by the OECD micro projects, as well as the European Union accession process, this analysis also confirms that difficulties with data collection and monitoring of SENDDD students are associated with poverty, discrimination and social stigma. A force field analysis using a three dimensional capacity analysis framework[7] is recommended to identify areas that need further clarification and future development for each country.

The opportunity to participate in another round of projects should be extended to the countries that have yet to be involved in this review process.

Identification

Guiding Questions

In most of the target countries, committees or boards identify (and "categorise") young children and students with disabilities/special needs. Please describe (1) the local distribution (numbers), (2) the structure (legal, organisational), (3) the concrete work of these categorisation committees, and (4) the mechanism under which these children are identified. (Table 6.1)

Please describe the categories used to identify young children and students with special education needs. What procedures are in place to monitor and eventually de-categorise these children? (Table 6.2)

How are young children and students with special education needs officially identified when they have not been registered by "categorisation committees"? What prevalence estimates would you expect, what groups (characteristics) would this cover and where would they have to be found? (Table 6.3)

Please describe the rights and responsibilities of young children and students with special education needs (and the parents of these children) who have been officially ascertained as having special education needs (financial support, services, pathways etc.). (Table 6.4)

Identification and classification

All economies have procedures for identifying and classifying children with disabilities and special educational needs. These procedures rely on multi-disciplinary categorisation committees that vary widely in membership, organisational structure and purpose.

Categorisation commissions and their distribution (numbers)

As can be seen in the column on local distribution in Table 6.1, categorisation committees often operate at two or more levels that vary between countries. In Bosnia and Herzegovina, committees are operated by cantons, and the Federal role is co-ordinating rather than overarching. In Latvia, there is an overarching State Pedagogical Medical Commission within a National Centre for Special Needs Education and 33 municipal pedagogical medical commissions appointed by local boards of education. In Serbia, there are 76 regional boards and 4 second level boards for classifying children with developmental problems.

Malta operates a Statementing Moderating Panel to establish the type and level of additional educational support needed by students with disabilities and special needs that is similar to the English national system in how it addresses identification and classification issues.

---

[7] See section on conclusions and recommendations for further explanation.

Table 6.1 **Identification - Categorisation Committees**

	Categorisation committee	Local distribution (numbers)	Legal structure	Organisational structure	Concrete work	Identification mechanisms
Estonia	Counselling Committee	One per county/city a total of 20	Regulations from Minister of Education	Multi-disciplinary including education staff and rep from local government	Committee can assign: a curriculum, a school or class, or postpone a decision	Decision of teacher's council. Can be initiated by class teacher or other professional with parents' consent
Latvia	State Pedagogical Medical Commission (SPMC) within National Centre for SNE	33 municipal PMCs (MPMC) appointed by local boards of education	Cabinet Ministers' Regulation (new Regulations are under review)	Multi-disciplinary. SPMC permanent basis- Most MPMC decisions April/May	Advises on appropriate curriculum and support	Pupils with problems are referred by class teacher to the council of teachers. There the decision is made what measures should be taken next in assessment of the child. Parent's consent compulsory.
Lithuania	School Special Needs Commission (SSNC) in first instance	Local Pedagogical Psychological Services (PPS) in most municipalities- second level	Within Law on Education (2003) and further law on assessment	Multi-disciplinary teams	Recommend special assistance/ modification to programme. Approved docs- time limited	Teacher referral. Referral to PPS after informing parents
Romania	Multiple agencies (ed, health, child protection, Handicap Authority). Child Protection Commissions	County/city level	Handicap rights laws & ed law	Under review by inter-ministerial group	Evaluation, enrolment and provision of special services	Under review
Bulgaria	Complex Pedagogical Assessment Teams (CPAT)	28 regional teams and resource centres	MOES-National programme for dev of sch. ed & integration	Multi-disciplinary	New guidelines for CPAT in 2007	Described in new guidelines

Table 6.1 **Identification - Categorisation Committees** (continued)

	Categorisation committee	Local distribution (numbers)	Legal structure	Organisational structure	Concrete work	Identification mechanisms
Moldova	Medical Psycho-Pedagogical Commission	National, regional municipal	National strategy on child and family protection	Under MOES but mostly medical professionals	Recommends ed. institution	Parents present-medical emphasis
Croatia	Two level structure-all children assessed on school entry	Every school has first level. Second level for each phase of schooling	Law on Elementary Education	Work in schools/social welfare on entry to school and throughout year	Multi disciplinary-recommends 'adequate schooling'	Every child assessed on entry to school
Bosnia and Herzegovina	Two level committee structure	Most municipalities have committees	Rule Book of Assessment of Ability	Multi-disciplinary	Observation, direct examination and documentation	Identification by various agencies & parents-expert teams-co-ordinated by centre for social work
Slovenia	SEN Guidance Commission	19	Guidance on Children with Special Needs	Multi-disciplinary (physician, psychologist & defectologists)	Commission sends prof statement to National Ed Inst. Which issues guidance order	Parents request national Ed Inst. which then asks SEN commission to assess/evaluate
Montenegro	Commission for Directing	18 out of 21 municipalities have commissions	Law on Special Needs	Commissions work in hospital	Proposal for 'directing' based on assessment consultation with educational institution	Request can from many sources including parents
Serbia	Board for Classifying Children with Developmental Problems	76 regional 4 second level Process under review	Law on Primary Education Rule Book	Multi-disciplinary-health dominated	Usually before start of primary school	Board examines and sends opinion to local gov. Children ascertained with SEN usually go to special school
Kosovo	Evaluation Committee (12 members)	Not reported	Law on primary & secondary education	12 members	See Box 6.1.	Parents and teachers can initiate and participate.
Malta	Statementing Moderating Panel	Statementing Moderating Panel is a nationally recognised body	Education Act 1988 (amended 2006) & Equal Ops Act 2000	Composed by educationalists including an educational psychologist	Functions clearly described on P3 of country report.	Panel works with Ch. Dev. Assessment Unit & SPS

Legal and organisational structure of the commissions

For the SEE economies and Baltic countries, the categorisation commissions that operated during the communist era still directly inform many of the arrangements and the assumptions upon which the commissions remain structured and governed. Prior to 1989, governments relied on large residential institutions to provide care to people with disabilities. Social welfare was characterised by a system of financial benefits and health care that was dependent upon state employment-related insurance categories. Disabled people received medical care and were either offered residential placements or cash benefits. The bureaucracy of this state system of social security required administrators to run and oversee it. In some economies, this has resulted in more than one type of commission: for example, educational commissions that decide educational placements, and social services commissions that decide the amount of welfare allowance and social care needs and may locate the child to places for special protection category of children. In other economies, one commission makes all decisions.

Regional commissions are appointed by the local government structure such as a municipality, county or *canton*. In some economies the commissions cover large geographical areas especially in rural areas where local expertise may not be available. The categorisation commissions are bound by specially designed regulations for this kind of work. The development of these guidelines or regulations may be under the authority of the Ministry of Education, Ministry of Health, the Ministry of Social Welfare or a combination of ministries. In all economies surveyed, the process operates within a legal framework and there may also be a 'Rulebook' of procedures. In some countries they are part of the law on education. In Bulgaria, for example, the Minister of Education and Science and the Regional Inspectorate for Education operate Complex Pedagogical Assessment Teams. The assessments can be also be made by the Complex Evaluation Service inside the Social Assistance and Child Protection Department from each county (*e.g.* in Romania). They are usually locally based, often within the local authority or municipality.

As noted above, the commissions consist of multidisciplinary teams, although in many countries health professionals dominate them. In SEE economies and Baltic countries, the categorisation commissions often consist of a medical doctor, a paediatrician, a psychologist, a defectologist, a social worker and a pedagogue. Except for Malta, where the Statementing Moderating Panel is concerned with the educational provision of children based on interdisciplinary assessment reports, the Country Reports expressed the view that these commissions are mainly concerned with medical aspects of child disability. The degrees of professional specialisation and sub-specialisations can vary according to country or type of disability. For example, a specialist dialectologist, such as surdopedagogue (hearing impairment) may be represented on the commission, as may a child psychologist or psychiatrist. In Kosovo, parents can invite a lawyer to take part in the proceedings of the categorisation commission.

The concrete work of classification committees

Categorisation commissions make identification decisions as well as decisions about benefits and services across a range of policy areas. Country Reports provided different degrees of detail and interpretation in the responses to this guiding question; however, in general, the assessments undertaken by categorisation commissions are used to secure additional funds for parents, decide school placements, disability allowances or any additional support. For example, the commission assesses the capacity of people with disabilities, under criteria that determine procedures of detection, assessment of ability, classification and registration of children and their physical and mental development. After an assessment is conducted a 'disability percentage', 'grade' or description of special needs may be applied. This administrative outcome is usually legal and it is often irreversible although parents generally have a right to appeal to a higher level commission.

Box 6.1 Concrete work of committees – Kosovo

The Kosovo Report describes the concrete work of the categorization committee:

Requests for evaluation will be sent to the chairman of the Evaluation Committee. Within 15 days of receiving the request for evaluation, the chairman will appoint a preparation meeting with permanent members of the Evaluation Committee to decide what kind of evaluation is needed, whereas in urgent cases this preparation meeting can be done electronically, by phone or by fax n. If needed, the Evaluation Committee has the right to ask for the needed documents in order to complete an objective and complete evaluation. Such a request carries the weight of a court order. Based on the evaluation results, the Committee decides on the provision of special services within the frame of regular education, such as: correction of speaking, additional hours of teaching, physiotherapy, language therapy, specialised instructions, medical help for children according to the type of disability, etc. the Committee also decides on the placement of the children in special classes, special school or in the most appropriate place for accommodating children with special needs.

The Committee for children's evaluation is required that within two months after receiving the request for evaluation, to complete the needed documentation with the needed data. The Committee chairman will supervise the process of execution of the decisions brought by the Committee.

The aim of these procedures is to assure special protection, education and life-skills training. Committees make educational placement decisions by assigning a child to a special school (class) or a mainstream school. They can recommend special services within mainstream education such as speech and language therapy, or additional hours of teaching or other support. However, even though pedagogues and special education teachers are represented on some commissions, the educational aspects of provision are mostly decided by professionals who have little experience of mainstream education. Moreover, in some economies, it is unclear whether any members of the commission would have first-hand knowledge of the child. Some commissions base their decisions only on paperwork; others assess the child themselves, however, these assessments could be criticised when evaluated against recent developments in childhood assessment procedures such as authentic assessment. For example, rarely does a commission assessment take place in a location known to the child, such as their home or school.

An exception to the above is found in the case of Malta where the members of the Statementing Moderating Panel are all educationalists. Here the chairperson is preferably an educational psychologist not professionally involved with the student being statemented. The Head of School or a representative is always invited by the panel to attend the statementing process of a particular student.

Box 6.2 **Objections to categorisation committees**

Dissatisfaction with the work of categorisation committees was expressed clearly in the Serbian Country Report which states that parents and other advocates were unhappy with the (old) arrangements because:

'Decisions are made based on one encounter with the child. Furthermore IQ tests are not standardised and are used uncritically. Due to socio-cultural insensitivities Roma children are often classified as intellectually disabled and recommended special schools. The board assessment is sometimes motivated by financial factors. If children are given higher level of disability they are likely to receive more support. Therefore pressures on Boards are known to happen.'

Dissatisfaction with categorisation committees has led some economies to initiate a reform of the commissions. Serbia and Romania are currently reviewing the work of their commissions. In Serbia it has been proposed that the name of the commission be changed to 'Board for Assessment and Guidance' to reflect a move towards a social model of disability in policy and practice. Other countries now have assessment procedures that are initiated by teachers and schools. In Croatia, every child is assessed on entry to school prior to any referral to a categorisation committee. Some arrangements permit parents to have a greater say in the process than would have been the case in the past.

The mechanisms under which these children are identified

As noted above, the procedures for categorisation are varied and can be initiated by social services, schools (teachers or head teachers), health services or parents and guardians. Children with severe or complex needs will often be identified prior to the school years as part the health check procedures of the country. However in some economies many disabled children do not come before the commissions and are not known to professionals due to stigma and prejudice associated with disability. Parents may see no benefits in bringing their (disabled) child to the notice of the authorities and may not even register the child's birth.

As is the case in many other countries of the world, children with less severe impairments are not identified as having SEN until they start school. In some countries (*e.g.* Croatia), every child goes through psychological assessment on entry to school. In other economies too, assessment boards and commissions operate at the school level.

It has been noted that the objectivity and reliability of the mechanisms under which children are identified is sometimes called into question because different classification teams within a country do not always use the same criteria. In response, Bulgaria developed 'Methodological Guidelines for the Activity of Complex Pedagogical Assessment Teams' (CPAT). The guidelines were developed and agreed by the specialists from different institutions and organisations in order to improve existing models of assessment and achieve a unified approach to identification. In Romania and Croatia, inter-ministerial groups are developing new guidelines. There is evidence that the practice of categorisation is changing in some economies, where the commissions are beginning to take into consideration social and educational needs of disabled children. For example, in Bulgaria the Complex Pedagogical Assessment Team makes the primary evaluation of the child's general development and suggests appropriate schooling and resource support. This team of specialists, a psychologist, speech and language therapist, special educational teacher, mainstream teacher and a doctor (medical psychiatrist or neurologist) is formed in the Regional Inspectorate for Education in each of the 28 regional towns in Bulgaria. The team evaluates the education needs of the disabled child and offers the parents, who are included in the ascertainment process, choices in education for their child in a mainstream or a special school. A mainstream teacher is part of the commission in Croatia and Kosovo. Parents can opt out of the assessment, but if they do they are not entitled to any resource provision or support.

Malta operates a 'Statementing Moderating Panel' that is focused on identifying special educational needs. The professional representation and functioning of the panel is similar to the process in England and reflects Malta's links with Britain.

Categories used to identify students with special educational needs

The term 'special educational needs' covers an array of problems from those related to particular impairments to those related to learning and behavioural difficulties experienced by some learners compared to other similar learners. The number of categories of special need varies between countries from three to ten (Table 6.2). Many economies use levels of severity from mild to severe (sometimes referred to as 'hard') to differentiate within categories. The categories always include sensory impairments (vision and hearing) and physical impairments. Most countries also include cognitive impairments, but these are described in different ways and may or may not include specific difficulties in learning such as dyslexia. Some have emotional, social and behavioural difficulties as a single category; others see them as separate and distinctive. Some countries have a category of communication disorders, which may or may not include speech and language difficulties. Sometimes autism is seen as a communication disorder. In SEE and the Baltic States, the term 'special needs' is often considered to mean children with physical or mental disabilities.

In some countries the use of these categories is mentioned as arising from the International Classification of Disability (ICD). More recent approaches that stress functioning, using the International Classification of Functioning, Disability and Health (ICF), are apparent in others. Micro projects in Bulgaria, Croatia, Serbia and Romania used approaches to categorisation informed by the OECD cross-national categories.

Table 6.2 **Identification categories and procedures used to identify children and students with special educational needs**

	Number of categories	Monitoring procedures	Procedures to de-categorise
Estonia	8 (including special talent and addiction disorder)	Yes	Not mentioned
Latvia	9	New Regulations of the Cabinet of Ministers determines the necessity to monitor and reassess special needs of pupils	After reassessment of the child the PMC can de-categorize the pupil. It is usually based on the evaluation report of the school and it can be initiated by child's parents
Lithuania	10	Yes	Yes
Romania	9 (four levels)	Yes	Annual review
Bulgaria	7 (under review)	Yes	Not mentioned
Moldova	Unclear 7 categories in institutions plus other social problems (19 ICD medical conditions examined in 2007)	Not mentioned	Not mentioned
Croatia	8 (under review)	Under review	Not mentioned
Bosnia and Hezergovina	7	Yes (periodic)	Yes
Slovenia	9 (including long-term ill)	Yes	Yes
Montenegro	9 disability categories plus sub-categories by levels of severity 31 in total	Yes	Yes
Serbia	4 in law (under review Micro project used 10)	Yes (under review)	Yes but seldom used (under review)
Kosovo	8	Yes	Triennial review
Malta	4 (mentioned in Education Act) Additional information on categories collected for statistical purposes	Yes	Yes

Monitoring and de-categorization procedures

In general, the country reports do not give a clear indication of the procedures for monitoring and de-categorising children, however in Malta, statement reviews must occur at key transition periods between phases of education and at age 14, or at anytime it is requested by one of the parties involved. As specified in Table 6.2, most economies specified that there were identification monitoring procedures in place – although fewer economies reported that there were procedures for the de-categorization of students once they have been identified as having special educational needs. The Romanian and Estonian Country reports specify that, once classified, children are continuously monitored. Romania reported an annual review process and Kosovo has adopted a process of triennial review. The extent to which these reviews take place and at what rate was not specified in the country reports. However, it is often the case that once categorised as having special education needs children are not regularly reassessed.

While there may be procedures to reassess or to de-classify students in policy, the available evidence suggests that once a label has been given it is not removed. Finally it should be noted there were some contradictions as to whether there were monitoring and de-classification procedures for each country in the documents reviewed for this report reaffirming the conclusion that there are gaps between policy and practice in this area.

Identification of children not registered by committees: prevalence and where found

Table 6.3 shows the country policy for the identification of children not registered by committees. The analysis of the country report highlights this as an area where there was a great deal of variability in practice and in interpretation. According to the OECD, *"those with special educational needs are defined by the additional public and/or private resources provided to support their education"* (OECD, 2005). It is interesting to note therefore that while most economies (with the exceptions of Bosnia and Herzegovina, Slovenia, Montenegro, and Serbia) were able to specify an identification policy, none provided prevalence estimates and few economies have developed systematic 'child find' mechanisms. Thus it is not possible to answer questions on prevalence estimates other than to use the European Academy of Childhood Disabilities population rate of 2.5% for disability (*e.g.* CNC A). It is interesting to note that the OECD mean is 2.6% for CNC A (2005) which, while not technically a prevalence estimate, is close to the European Academy figure. It is also worth noting that individual OECD member countries deviate considerably from this figure.[8] The use of such benchmarks should be helpful in countries where disabled children are known to be unregistered due to the stigma associated with disability.

This is an important area for future work as reported prevalence rates are often interpreted as a formal recognition of disability. While disability registers record the number of children who have been issued certificates by categorisation commissions as a prerequisite for claiming benefits, the number of children with disabilities whose families do not claim benefits and those who are not in school is unknown. This is further complicated by the unknown number of children with disabilities living in institutions who are not included in disability registers, as well as children residing in special institutions who are not disabled.

---

[8] In 2005, in the United States there were 5.57% of students in CNC A in compulsory education while in Japan the equivalent figure was 1.64%

Table 6.3 **Identification - Special Needs**

	SEN identification policy	Prevalence	Where found
Estonia	Special educational needs may be identified by schools for targeted intervention prior to a referral to the Counselling Committee		
Latvia	Child only considered to have special educational needs if assessed by PMC The adopted Regulations of the cabinet of Ministers determines that pupils could be identified by specialists in schools and should have support measures without assessment of PMC		
Lithuania	Special educational needs are identified by school special needs commission for targeted intervention prior to a referral to the local pedagogical/psychological service		
Romania	Initial identification of SEN by a doctor, the child's parents or the school. Evaluation and certification carried out by the Complex Evaluation Service		
Bulgaria	Special educational needs assessed by Complex Pedagogical Assessment Teams		
Moldova	Uses the language of child rights but policies on identification still in development. A Medical/Psycho/Pedagogical Council has been created.		
Croatia	School level committees screen all children on entry to school and monitor progress throughout school year.		
Bosnia and Herzegovina	Discovery by parents, health, educational and social work institutions. Expert committees assess abilities and determine support. They also identify and categorise SEN. Not all municipalities have these committees		
Slovenia	Carried out by the ministries of Health and Education,		
Montenegro	Process starts with a request from parents or various agencies to local authority, which informs commission. Not all SEN children are known about.		
Serbia	Under review – currently every child goes through psychological assessment on entry to school, but the information is held by the school		
Kosovo	Under review - glossary of terms used by diagnostic centres		
Malta	Four categories as defined in education law see Table 6.2	2.5%	

Rights and responsibilities

Country reports varied with respect to how the guiding question pertaining to rights and responsibilities for students with special educational needs was addressed. Table 6.4 provides some indication of this variability. All economies have some form of rights-based legislation that covers people with disabilities but these varied from anti-discrimination policies to educational rights and/or child protection laws. It is not possible to say whether countries that reported education legislation as a form of rights under this section did or did not also have anti-discrimination and child protection laws. In Malta, one of the duties of the Child Commissioner is to promote and advocate for the rights and interests of children.

Careful reading of the country reports suggests that the specification of rights and responsibilities in terms of financial supports, services and pathways is complicated by differing interpretations. In Bulgaria, some children with special educational needs are not entitled to support, but a new education act will soon revise the categories of special educational need, so that more children will be entitled to additional support in schools and communities. The Country Report for Estonia provides details on what is available in schools, such as: remedial classes, individual curriculum, smaller classes, adapted study materials (Braille, sign language interpreter). The Kosovo Report specifies what support should be in place, but it does not give evidence of this happening in practice. In Serbia, students with special educational needs are exempt from entrance exams in secondary schools, however they are also more likely to attend special secondary schools in the first instance. Lithuania's system is different from other countries and economies included in this report because it operates on a per capita basis referred to as a 'pupil basket model' whereby money follows the pupil. This money can be used for staff, textbooks and teaching aids. A student with special educational needs is entitled to a 'basket' of resources 33% more than that available to other students.

There is a trend for parents to be more actively involved in the decision making process as a result of the enactment of rights-based legislation. Some country reports mention responsibility of parents, which is usually to send a child to a school. However, as can be seen by the number of blank cells in Table 6.4, very little information was provided in the country reports about rights and responsibilities. Evidence was sometimes found in the report of the follow-up visits suggesting that additional guidance might be necessary in order to obtain accurate information about this area.

Table 6.4 **Identification - rights and responsibilities**

	Rights	**Financial support**	**Services**	**Pathways**	**Other**
Estonia	Yes	Yes	Yes		Smaller classes
Latvia	Yes	Yes	Yes		
Lithuania	Yes	Yes	Yes	Partial	
Romania	Yes	Yes	Yes	No	
Bulgaria	Yes	Yes		No	
Moldova	Yes				Difficult to assess
Croatia	Yes	Yes	Yes	Partial	
Bosnia and Herzegovina	Yes	Yes		No	
Slovenia	Yes	Yes (guidance)		No	
Montenegro	Yes	Partial	Yes	Yes (range of services)	
Serbia	Yes (under review)	Partial	Partial	Partial	
Kosovo	Yes				Braille
Malta	Yes	Parents of children with severe disabilities receive a special allowance	Yes	Yes	

The reports generally do not state whether parents have any rights such as flexible employment, financial support, respite care, or help with the child care. However, the country reports for Bosnia and Malta provide a list of other available services such as free health care, financial support by Centres of Social Work and medical aids. In Malta, the parents of children attending independent private schools, and who need the support of a learning assistant, benefit from income tax relief. Children who live in residential institutions receive different services from those who are in residential schools or mainstreams schools. All reports say that children with special needs have rights to equal access to education and about half the reports say that SEN children have a right to attend and receive support in regular schools. However to what extent this right is exercised is not clear except in the Malta report which states that 88% of students with statements attend mainstream schools.

Data flow

Guiding Questions

Which Ministries (and/or governmental and non governmental agencies) are regularly involved in gathering data on young children and students with special education needs? What kind of data do they collect (criteria, target groups) and when? (Table 6.5)

In what way and under what regulations do these institutions work together? Please describe the flow of information and barriers to formal/informal collaboration on data exchange on young children and students with special education needs. (Table 6.6)

Data gathering: who, what and when?

All economies collect data on young children and students with special educational needs but there is variation within and across countries with respect to the kinds of data collected. Ministries of education gather information on children with special needs who are enrolled in the education system. Ministries of health collect data on childhood disability, ministries of social welfare or social protection may have data on children who receive disability benefits or because they are in special institutions. In some economies, non-governmental organisations (NGOs) and international agencies also collect data on vulnerable children, but these data tend to pertain to specific projects or groups of children or particular areas.

As shown in Table 6.5 the country report responses to this guiding question all specified that education ministries (variously described as education, ministry of education, ministry of education and science, ministry of education, science and technology) were regularly involved in gathering data. Some country reports also included reference to other agencies' data collection activities but this does not imply that only these economies involve multiple agencies in these activities. It is possible that the question was interpreted by some to include all data collected on disability issues, while others interpreted the question more narrowly to pertain to educational needs only.

Country reports for Estonia and Malta (see Box 6.3) included descriptions of comprehensive data collection systems. The Estonian Information System for Education (EISE) is an electronic data base that consolidates information on all pupils included in the education system. This includes data on type of placement (mainstream, special class or special school), type of individual support, form of study, curriculum, pupils who need, but do not get special support, type of support system/study support and subjects where students get individual support. Other economies collect information on the number of students by placement. Many reported problems with data reliability, reaffirming this as a key challenge for the development of sound national data collection systems.

Table 6.5 **Which Ministries (and or governmental and NGOs) are involved in gathering data, what kinds of data do they collect and when?**

	Ministries	NGOs	Type of data	When collected	Notes
Estonia	Education		Placement Supports resources	regularly	EISE data system
Latvia	MOES Ministry of Welfare	SUSTENTO-umbrella organization for NGOs	Demographic-Curriculum placement	Start of school year	Regulation National statistics education
Lithuania	Dept of Statistics; Health & SS; MOES		Categorical as required by each ministry. Educational data by school	regularly	Working party reviewing types of data
Romania	MOES	RENINCO	Placement medical	Not specified	See micro report
Bulgaria	MOE RIE(inspectorate) CPAT SACP (State Agency of Child Protection), and NSI (National Statistical Institute)	Yes (NGOs of and for people with disabilities)	Demographic resource	Start of school year by school	LIST model of schools
Moldova	MOE				Date base from residential institutions
Croatia	MoSES Ministry of Public Health and Social Welfare Ministry of Family, Veterans and Integration Solidarity	NGOs of and for people with disabilities Professional NGOs	Various, numerous		Multiple types of data collected
Bosnia and Herzegovina	MOE Min Work & Soc policy		By school demographic	2 x per year	'SEN' not category dropout language
Slovenia	MOE; MOS Health Labour and Social Welfare	Yes	Not unified - hard to distinguish	Statistical office	NGO & Gvt agencies do not share data considered unreliable
Montenegro	MOES	Yes, for some tertiary	By institution		data considered unreliable
Serbia	MOE	Project data	Placement	Start of school year	Dept for Infomatics and Ed Stats in MOE and Institute fro Improvement of Education and Upbringing
Kosovo	MEST	Project data	Demographic	Start of school year	Statistics Office of Kosovo
Malta	MOE; MOH Family Affairs[1]		Demographic various numerous	Regularly	National Statistics Office

Note: In 2009 these Ministries were consolidated into the Ministry for Social Policy.

As can be seen from Table 6.5, there are a variety of data collected in different economies. While some countries collect information on type of disability, placement, age, gender, school level, other countries have placement data on the numbers of children in different forms of provision (special or mainstream). These data are often collected and reported by placement of the child rather than by type of disability. For example, in Bulgaria there are different lists for children in mainstream and children in special schools. The Serbian report states that a number of children with special needs are enrolled in regular schools without being registered as having special needs. Thus, data collection by type of placement creates particular problems of data reliability for many countries.

In addition to problems of data reliability, there are also issues of which data to collect. It will be important to aim for consensus on this question as countries develop and invest in improved data collection efforts.

How do institutions work together?

Flow of information

Countries varied with respect to whether there were interagency agreements or regulations to support the sharing of information in place. The Estonian Information System on Education is maintained pursuant to data protection and education laws. Accuracy of information provided by educational institutions is monitored by state supervision. Other economies had agreements but identified gaps in information or in policy implementation. In Bosnia and Herzegovina, cantonal ministries of education have a duty to communicate data to the Federal Ministry of Education and to the Ministry of Civil Affairs but the cantons do not agree on the types of data that should be collected or shared. Croatia has a register of people with disabilities but reported that methods of data collection are often incompatible. According to the Kosovo report, the institutions that collect data work together through published reports and specific requests for data exchange.

Malta (see Box 6.3) and Estonia have comprehensive and technically sophisticated data collection systems, supported by data protection legislation with clear division of responsibility among ministries and offices. Bulgaria is moving in a similar direction with new software coming on stream. These are important developments that are essential to the flow of information between agencies. A number of countries have national statistics agencies that routinely collect data from across different ministries. Such agencies have the potential to bring together different ministries so that data on vulnerable children might be shared.

Box 6.3 **Data collection system in Malta**

In Malta, the Directorate of Education within the Ministry of Education, Culture, Youth, and Sport collects data from individual schools at the beginning of every school year. These data include information on children with special needs. The Inclusive Education Branch within the Directorate for Educational Services collates micro-data for children with special needs in mainstream schools.

The Maltese National Statistics Office (NSO) collates data for all mainstream schools on age, sex, class promoted/repeated status, days of absence, disability types, etc. The NSO annual publication 'Education Statistics' includes a section on special education including type of disability, age, schools level and place of schooling. When students are assessed by the Child Development Assessment Unit a report is given to parents who decide whether to forward the report to other ministries or education authorities. When the child moves from school to adult centre for persons with disabilities the personal file is transferred with parental consent. The Ministry of Social Policy is responsible for collecting and updating all data necessary for issuing the Disabled Child Allowance. The Ministry of Social Policy collates data regarding congenital anomalies, changes in occurrence of congenital anomalies, fatalities and provides data for epidemiological studies nationally and internationally, in accordance with Data Protection Act from 2001.

Barriers to formal/informal collaboration

The country reports identified many barriers to collaboration in the exchange of data on young children and students with special educational needs. For some there are no regulations under which agencies work together. For others, data protection laws were cited as preventing the sharing of information. For example, personnel from education sometimes do not have an access to databases of social services or health. As a consequence few countries have intergovernmental data sets that are compatible.

Many country reports gave details of difficulties with communication and networking between ministries and other agencies. These barriers to sharing information are associated with a range of problems including those that arise from: an absence of agreed definitions and shared terminology; incompatible computer software that does not allow data to be shared; insufficient computer capacity, especially at the local level; a shortage of adequately trained professionals working on the task; disputes between regions/municipalities and professional mistrust that is sometimes linked to differences in perceived status.

However despite these problems, there a number of developments, for example in Estonia, that suggest these barriers are being addressed. In addition, the OECD Micro-Projects have provided support for these efforts.

Table 6.6 **Data flow - working together**

	Interagency agreement/regulations in place	Type of information shared	Barriers to collaboration
Estonia	Yes		Gaps in content of data between Education and Social Services
Latvia	Ministry of Welfare National Bureau of Statistics	Disability demographic	Yes lack of co-operation between ministries
Lithuania	Dept of Statistics		Co-operation good but system under developed
Romania	Not clear	various	Many barriers identified
Bulgaria	Yes	comprehensive	None mentioned
Moldova	No		Different ministerial responsibilities for children with disabilities & education
Croatia	Croatian register for People with Disabilities		Methods of data collection often incompatible
Bosnia and Herzegovina	No Laws on statistics	none	Canton disputes
Slovenia	Statistical Office	none	Data protection limits sharing
Montenegro	No - legal framework does not exist		Poor data flow working on development of software
Serbia	No information – data protection limits sharing	None	Ministries are not working together Ministries of Welfare, Health and Education have departments of statistics but there are no interagency agreements for data sharing
Kosovo	Data not systematic		Statistics Office Kosovo
Malta	Regular data flow between education and NSO. Also from special schools to Adult Centres within Ministry of Social Policy	various	

Monitoring

Guiding Questions

Please describe the legal framework in which data collection and monitoring of people with disabilities is taking place. (Table 6.7)

In what ways are data on students with SEN covered by official education statistics? Please, describe the main actors, concrete mechanisms and categories used in official school statistics. Differentiate between pre-school education, compulsory education, upper secondary education and tertiary education, if possible. (Table 6.8)

Transition to employment and/or institutions of tertiary education: in what ways are pathways of students with special education needs measured when they have finished compulsory (and/or) secondary schooling? (Table 6.9)

Is there any statistical information on school abandonment or dropout rates for young children and students with special education needs? (Table 6.10)

Please give the most recent data on young children and students with special education needs in regular classes, special classes, special schools and special institutions. Please include early education and care and institutions of tertiary education in this overview. (Table 6.11)

There was some confusion in the country reports about how to report monitoring. This may have arisen from confusion between monitoring of individual children and monitoring of data at the regional or national level.

Legal frameworks

Not all reports state under which regulations data are collected, but some do and these are specified in Table 6.7. Reports from countries that are members of the European Union tend to emphasise children's rights and national legislation. In Bulgaria data collection is regulated by the Education Act and Child Protection Act. The Romanian report provides comprehensive analysis and data on children with special needs and emphasises children's rights in national legislation. The Estonian Information System on Education is maintained and operates according to a Databases Act, the Personal Data Protection Act, the Education Act of Estonian Republic and statutes of the system. The Serbian country report states that the Rulebook on Classification Criteria for Children with Disabilities is the only legal document that regulates data collection. The Bosnian country report states that data collection is governed by the law on statistics at the level of state and the level of entity. In Bosnia and Herzegovina there is no national data collection according to categories of difficulties because there is no unified law on the rulebook of categorisation of children with special needs.

Table 6.7 **Monitoring - legal framework**

Estonia	Data Protection
Latvia	Regulations for data protection
Lithuania	Regulated by government
Romania	National institute for statistics Multiple agencies collect data - not complete
Bulgaria	National Statistics Institute Data Protection and Education Laws
Moldova	No information provided
Croatia	Data Protection
Bosnia and Herzegovina	SEN not legally defined at the federal level – however entity and cantonal decisions have legal status in terms of the right to support
Slovenia	No information provided
Montenegro	No information - legal definition for data protection does not exist
Serbia	No legal definition
Kosovo	No information provided
Malta	Data Protection Act. The Malta Statistics Authority Act and the Education Act

---

Box 6.4 **Bulgarian micro report and legal framework**

The micro report and the country report from Bulgaria provide detailed analysis and information on children with special needs. The report contains a number of tables with data on special schools segregated by type of school, the resource centres and the number of children supported by the resource centres. Furthermore the report compares national categories against OECD categories of SENDDD. The Bulgarian reports on a pilot project from ten regular schools. The highest percentage of resource support in mainstream schools is for children with 'mental retardation'. The report also identifies how many children are included in what stages of education and where the problems are in the education system. A detailed analysis on special educational needs with strong emphasis on legislative acts is provided. In Bulgaria the following policies relate to education of children with special needs: the National Programme for development of school education and pre-school education and preparation (2006-2015), People's Education Act, Rules for the Application of the People's Education Act, National Plan for the Integration of Children with Special Education Needs and/or with Chronic Diseases, Handicapped People Integration Act. These policies are based on the legislative EU framework, the UN education documents, the Salamanca Declaration and Framework of Action for Special Education, 1994; the Dakar framework of Action, 2000.

Special educational needs and education statistics

Table 6.8 displays information about school statistics and special educational needs. All countries and economies except for Moldova and Lithuania reported that data on special educational need were monitored in education statistics. However, the number of categories used and the extent to which data were collected by sector (preschool, compulsory, upper secondary and tertiary) were variable. Some economies reported that data were available by sector but did not provide it, others provided numbers but not percentages, others provided percentages but it was unclear to what the percentage referred. Given that the age at which students are enrolled in the various sectors of education, and the extent to which the ages and years of compulsory schooling vary between countries, it is not possible to make judgments about the extent to which the data are comparable. As a result, Table 6.8 simply provides an indication of the kind of information that was included in the country reports.

Table 6.8 **Monitoring - School statistics and SEN**

	Data on SEN in education statistics?	**Categories used for monitoring**	**Preschool**	**Compulsory**	**Upper secondary**	**Tertiary**
Estonia	Yes	8	Yes	Yes	Yes	Yes
Latvia	Yes	9	Yes	Yes	There is data about pupils with visual, hearing impairments and physical disabilities	Partial - Vocational Ed, Data about higher education currently being compiled
Lithuania	Yes	10	Yes	Yes	Yes	Yes
Romania	Partial	Not reported		Yes	Not reported	Not reported
Bulgaria	Yes sophisticated	9 (using CNC)	Yes	Yes	Yes	Yes
Moldova	No	Not reported	No	Yes number	Not reported	Not reported
Croatia	Yes	Moving to CNC	Yes No. & %	Yes Number & %	Yes Number & %	Yes Number & %
Bosnia and Herzegovina	Yes	13 for monitoring	Yes Number & %	Yes Number & %	Yes Number & %	Not reported
Slovenia	Yes	9	Yes Number	Yes Number	Yes	Yes Monitor
Montenegro	Yes	No (only special or regular)	Yes Number & %	Yes Number & %	Not reported	
Serbia	Yes	11 categories used for monitoring (micro-report)	Not reported but some indication of %	Yes-total number	Not reported	Not reported but some indication of Number
Kosovo	Yes	8	Yes Number	Yes number	Yes Number	?
Malta	Yes	7 categories for statistical purposes	Yes but Not reported			

In classifying children with disabilities most economies use categories that correspond with the cross national category 'A' (organic, motor or neurological disorders). When levels of severity are included, Montenegro has 31 categories, including children with long-term diseases. All of the categories used in Montenegro come under the Cross National Category (CNC) 'A'. In Croatia, Bulgaria and Romania include those within CNC 'B' (learning difficulties, behavioural, emotional or specific learning difficulties).

As a result of the Micro-project reports, it was possible to see evidence of how some economies were beginning to monitor special educational needs according to the cross-national categorisation system. Where this was the case, for example, in Bulgaria, the categories used by the committees were predominately in CNC 'A' while CNC 'B' and CNC 'C' (learning difficulties that arise from socio-economic, cultural or linguistic factors) became new categories.

However, more clarification is needed on what constitutes learning disability, since this term appears in the country reports. Learning disability is sometimes used instead of 'intellectual disability' and sometimes for specific learning difficulties such as dyslexia, or dyscalculia. Children from culturally or linguistically different backgrounds, such as Roma children, are sometimes erroneously classified as having learning disabilities which results in their being classified and counted in CNC 'A' when assignment to CNC 'C' would be more accurate.

Box 6.5 **Education of disadvantaged children - Roma**

One of the accession criteria that EU candidate countries need to fulfill is to address discrimination and exclusion of Roma people. Major Roma communities live across SEE countries, however they suffer from severe social and cultural exclusion. OECD supported research in Hungary found that Roma children are overrepresented in special education and often segregated in separate classes. The research found Roma children to be among the most educationally disadvantaged children in the region (Csányi, 2008). The Serbian country report states that Roma children are uncritically classified as mentally disabled and placed in special school due to being socio-culturally and educationally neglected. Also the research on Roma children education by the NGO Budimo Aktivni from Bosnia and Herzegovina suggests that the high level of exclusion is caused not only by the severe poverty and illiteracy of Roma, but also because schools are rarely able to cope with their educational needs. According to this research, around 80% of Roma children in Bosnia and Herzegovina who are not in school want an education (UNICEF, 2006). However, the countries of South East Europe are trying to improve the situation for Roma through different polices and plans of action. In Bosnia and Herzegovina the National Plan of Action for Education of Roma and other National Minorities (OSCE, 2004) stresses needs for increased financial support with the free provision of school books and transport for Roma and introduction of Roma language in schools.

Transition to adulthood

As is the case in many countries around the world, school age students with disabilities are entitled to education and additional support services, but there is generally no similar entitlement to adult services. As a result, many countries are increasingly recognising the need for policies to support people with disabilities make transitions from school to adult life. However, the first issue young people with disabilities face when leaving school is determining whether or not they are eligible for continued services as adults, and if so, which services might be available. Not only are there limited pathways open to people with disabilities, but also the paths are not always clearly signposted, and few data are available to map them. As can be seen in Table 6.9, very little data has been collected to monitor pathways available to assist students with disabilities when they finish compulsory or secondary schooling.

Table 6.9 **Monitoring – transition**

	Are pathways monitored	How/when	By whom	Other
Estonia	No			
Latvia	Partial			Data on grads from compulsory ed, number in voc. ed.
Lithuania	No			
Romania	Partial			Those who pass exams & go to university
Bulgaria	Partial (pilot info)			
Moldova	No			
Croatia	Yes		Croatian Employment Service	
Bosnia and Herzegovina	No			
Slovenia	No			
Montenegro	No			
Serbia	Partial monitoring by NGOs and Ministry			
Kosovo	Partial			
Malta	Described			Monitoring unclear Special courses at college

School abandonment and dropout

Few countries covered in this review systematically collect data on enrolment, completion and dropout for students with special educational needs (Table 6.10). However, it is not clear whether participating economies understood this question in the same way, because there are no clear definitions what these terms mean. School abandonment is often associated with poverty, early motherhood, discrimination and child labour. In Romania for example, abandonment is discussed in relation to Roma children. On the other hand, dropout appears to be related to conditions in school, such as poor staffing levels and poor teacher training.

In Bulgaria, the Ministry of Education and Science collects data on student dropout from the education system, however these data do not contain information on students with special needs who drop out. Malta operates the 'Good Shepherd Programme' by which the school enrolment is checked against the government's common database.

Table 6.10 **Monitoring – school abandonment and dropout rates**

	School abandonment	**Drop out rates**	**Notes**
Estonia	No data reported	0.8%	National rate includes SEN
Latvia	Data not collected		
Lithuania	Data not collected		
Romania			Estimated 80% dropouts have SEN
Bulgaria		3.1%	National rate includes SEN
Moldova	No data reported		
Croatia	No data reported		Do not have relevant data
Bosnia and Herzegovina		Available?	Not reported
Slovenia	No data available	3.8%	Data refer to children in basic education attending special schools or special institutions for children with SEN
Montenegro	Data not currently collected but procedures are being developed		
Serbia			Data collected by not specific to SEN
Kosovo	Data not collected		
Malta			Data available indirectly in promotion and retention stats, not specific to SEN

Placement data for children and young people with special educational needs

There seem to be an ambiguity in country reports and micro reports in **interpreting** the final guiding question. This is attributed to differing understandings of what constitutes special institutions. It is not clear from the country reports whether and how jurisdictions differentiated between special schools and special institutions. Often the placement data do not distinguish between special schools and special institutions. Thus it is difficult to distinguish between those who are in residential provision and those who are in day (special) schools. Few economies have data at the level of the individual child which contains demographic details (for example; age, gender, language spoken, ethnicity, address, etc. together with their SEN status and other educational information such as attainment scores and levels of support provided. Table 6.11 provides a summary of the available information.

Table 6.11 **Monitoring - school placement numbers of children by type of setting**

	Regular classes	Special classes	Special schools	Special institutions	Source	Notes
Estonia	19 270 11.7%	1 426 0.9%	3 720 2.3%		Country report	2006/07 data percent of population
Latvia	1 473	1 140	8 336	Included in the given data	Country report	2006/07 data (total number of pupils in day schools 266 111)
Lithuania	51 970 88.1%	906 1.4%	5 600 10.5%		Country report	2006/07 data of children with SEN
Romania			27 445		Country report	2006/07 data 20 728 Total no. SEN mnstrm school
Bulgaria	432 SEN in pilot regular schools				Country report	Data not aggregated
Moldova				10 091 (includes orphanages, etc)	Country and Micro reports	2005/06 data Number in 63 special institutions
Croatia			3 036		Country report	No year 54 961 Total no. SEN mnstrm school
Bosnia and Herzegovina (Tuzla canton)	5 673 7.2%	46	171		Country report	No year CNC categories percent of population
Slovenia	7 123	151	2 233	1006	Statistical Office	Under special institutions are also included social-health care centres for children with severe and profound mental disabilities
Montenegro	1 591 elem only			443	Country report	No year
Serbia	18 032	3 715	7 165		Country report	2006/07 data from a sample of 50 mainstream schools suggest 11% of total population
Kosovo						2006/07 data 899 in special schools and attached classes
Malta			277 0.5%			1 907 Total no. SEN in mnstrm schs (3.5% of population). 88% of students with statements in mnstrm schools. 123 in Malta College of Arts Science and Technology

Conclusion and recommendations

This chapter identifies key areas for action arising from the country situation analysis. These are discussed in terms of the conceptual, technical and legal issues that should be considered when developing new forms of national datasets that can be convertible for use by international organisations such as *e.g.* OECD, European Commission, UNESCO, and World Bank. Recommendations are made to improve data collection and quality so that important questions about participation in education for different groups of children may be answered.

The country reports reviewed as part of this process indicate many variations in the ways in which children are classified and in how data are collected. They also provide evidence of significant change and development in many countries. The variations in responses from each of the countries to the guiding questions are sometimes difficult to interpret. In some cases the data needed to answer the question were not available; in other cases it was not clear whether the data were not available or not provided. It is also possible that some of the questions were not understood. Thus the findings presented here should be interpreted as partial, subject to further information gathering activities and confirmation by the participating economies.

Eight of the countries in this review took part in a micro-project based on the introduction of the OECD cross-national categories 'A' (disability), 'B' (difficulties), and 'C' (disadvantage). There is evidence in the micro-reports that this process has been helpful in producing useful data for monitoring and comparison purposes. For example in Bulgaria, innovations make it possible to have more specific information about students who are described as having 'special educational needs'. Data about children can now be collected across a range of demographic and educational variables and at a variety of levels from the individual to the national. Developments in computer technology now make it relatively easy for information about individual children to be aggregated to the school, the local, and then to the national level. Such systems have the potential to improve the quality of monitoring and accountability as well as providing important data for national and cross-national comparisons.

However, technological advances alone will not improve the quality or usefulness of the data. This will require greater clarity of ***purpose.*** Data are collected for a variety of purposes, including classification, monitoring the progress of individuals, auditing the allocation of resources, monitoring standards at the school, local and national level, and in the context of this review, reviewing the educational participation of vulnerable groups of children. Different purposes require different types of data, collected at different levels and at different times.

In addition, there needs to be consideration of three other areas, each associated with barriers to the collection and sharing of data. These areas are: *conceptual, technical* and *legal.*

Conceptual issues

Conceptual issues include problems associated with identification, classification and categorisation and also with how the different demographic and educational variables might be defined. Some forms of disability and difficulty have relatively clear diagnostic criteria particularly those in cross-national category 'A'. Sometimes such difficulties are referred to as 'normative'. Sensory impairment would be a good example, as it is possible to measure visual and hearing acuity. Where impairments and disabilities are 'non-normative', then it becomes even more difficult to have precise definitions and therefore less easy to decide whether a child should (or should not) be classified as disabled or having a special educational need. Educational needs are changeable, open to interpretation and very often context specific. Whilst recent moves towards social and interactive models of disability have been welcomed, it has to be recognised that members of minority groups are often inappropriately identified as disabled or as having special educational needs.

Sometimes the terms disability and special educational need are used synonymously. And yet it is widely accepted that it is possible to have a disability and not a special educational need and it is possible to have a special educational need and not have a disability. Many economies reported numbers and percentages of children in different forms of provision. Thus categories tell us as much about where a child is being educated as they do about a child's disability or special need. This is important because in many countries the data says less about a child's difficulties, more about the provision they receive and where they receive it. Thus a child becomes a child with a learning difficulty when they are located in provision for children with learning difficulties. In such cases, the data therefore reports the availability of provision, which may or may not relate to the prevalence of a disability.

In response to the lack of specificity in the SEN data, in part because of moves to be less categorical, some countries also collect additional pupil level data for statistical purposes (Malta). One consequence of having a larger number of categories of 'special educational needs' may mean less information rather than more. Allocation of children to one of this larger group of categories will inevitably be subject to inaccuracy and over-simplification in ways that more precise categories such as age and gender, are not. The adoption of these categories may lead to more detailed, but not necessarily, more consistent information about how students are described as having 'special educational needs' for monitoring and accountability purposes.

Technical issues

Technical issues have to do with the structure of the data sets themselves, the extent to which they are 'complete', who is responsible for entering and collecting the data, how the data are shared, what analyses are possible and the robustness and flexibility of the computer software on which they operate. Although national databases aim to be comprehensive, they can only be as reliable as the data provided. In many economies, not all children are in the system. Few countries mentioned procedures to find 'missing' children. However, there are 'invisible and missing' children who might never have been registered in the first instance. This is a real issue in economies where stigma and shame are associated with disability, particularly where there are no benefits associated with registration and no penalties for non-registration. In some economies, minority groups do not participate in censuses, birth registration and other forms of data collection. Further, there are relatively large numbers of pupils for whom there are missing data, especially pupils with SEN. This can partly be explained by mobility, migration and refugee status. It may also be a function of exclusion in its various forms. An important aspect of this task therefore is to address the issue of the missing children. It is hard to provide services for children who are not known about.

Several countries report problems with hardware availability and software compatibility between the different computer systems used in different ministries. Sometimes schools do not have the necessary computer capacity to collect all the data that might be helpful.

Changes in policy and practice in many countries regarding the identification and assessment of students with SEN will result in changes to the type of data that are available to be collected. It will also expand the range of professionals who might be involved in the process. Clearly there is the need for professional development in relation to the classification process as well as support to develop systems for the handling and sharing of the data.

Technical issues arising from the nature of the data including problems associated with working with incomplete or partial samples should be addressed when considering the types of data collected. In addition, countries collect different types of data: nominal data such as types of disability; and/or ordinal data such levels of severity. It is important to remember that categories of SEN imply nominal level data from which only limited comparisons between classes (*e.g.* intellectual disabilities, visual impairment) can be made. While it is possible to compare the numbers of children and young people in various categories, it is not possible to determine level of need within the categories without additional ordinal or interval level data. However, it is difficult to secure professional agreement in determining appropriate ordinal or interval measures

Further there are difficulties in sharing data that may be 'vertical'. Such problems arise when aggregating from the level of the child, to the school, to the local and then to the national. Other problems may be 'horizontal'. These occur when schools do not pass on information about children when they change school or when ministries do not communicate with each other for various reasons, including professional mistrust, a lack of understanding about matters of disability, privacy and data protection laws (see below).

In addition, some economies cite incompatible software as a reason for difficulties in sharing data across ministries. However, the most fundamental problem relates to the quality and availability of the data itself. Data cannot be shared if it does not exist.

Legal

Legal barriers arise when considering how the data are to be used, who 'owns' the data and with the regulations that permit or restrict data flow between, for example, the various agencies of local and national government. In most countries there are data protection and privacy laws, which govern the ways in which data can be collected and used. In certain cases this can mean that important information about children is not shared between the different agencies of government. Whilst the protection of privacy is vital, the experience of other countries shows that it is possible to develop systems for sharing data while safeguarding privacy.

Recommendations

While there is no single recommendation for improving data flow and monitoring systems that applies to all economies, the country reports indicated high levels of awareness and urgency to improve data collection systems. In some economies, the lack of electronic databases and trained staff is a clear problem. Communication between different bodies and ministries also undermines data flow and monitoring. In order **to identify areas that need further clarification and future development**, a force field analysis using the three dimensional capacity analysis framework outlined below could provide a tool for supporting countries to develop a programme of work for making further improvements to their national data collection and monitoring systems:

	Identification	Data Flow	Monitoring
Conceptual			
Technical			
Legal			

Improvements in data collection efforts were clearly achieved in those economies that participated in the OECD micro projects. All countries can build on the lessons learned from these projects. The opportunity to participate in another round of projects should be extended to the countries that have yet to undertake a micro project. Those who have had projects should be supported in further interagency work between ministries and different professional groups on how to build reliable and useful datasets.

The **collection of data that can be convertible using the OECD framework** will require on-going technical assistance. Developments in data handling mean that more data can be collected across a range of levels from the individual child to the national level. This raises questions about the need for greater clarity of purpose and consideration of which data should be collected at each of the different levels. It may require revision of established categories that have legal standing, as well as the adoption of new definitions of disability. Professional development and technical assistance in the form of seminars and workshops, supported with widely distributed printed material on developments on disability classification in education can support these recommendations.

References

Csányi, Yvonne (24 June 2008), personal email communication: Ministry of Education statistics on the segregation of disadvantaged and Roma in Hungary.

OECD (2005), *Equity in Education: Students with Disabilities, Difficulties and Disadvantages*, Paris: OECD.

OSCE (2004), Action Plan on the Educational Needs of Roma and Other National Minorities in Bosnia and Herzegovina: http://www.oscebih.org/documents/80-eng.pdf, retrieved, 24 July 2008.

UNICEF, not dated; Bosnia and Herzegovina: new data reveal barriers to Roma education: http://www.unicef.org/ceecis/reallives_3635.html, Retrieved 24 July 2008.

UNICEF (2005), "Children and Disability in Transition in CEE/CIS and Baltic States". Florence: Innocenti Insight Centre.

Chapter 7. PISA 2006 and the Participation of Students with Special Educational Needs[9,10]

Interest in the inclusion of students with special educational needs in mainstream education has increased faster than the actual inclusion of these students in standardised assessment and accountability systems. This chapter discusses the participation and performance of students with special education needs in the Baltic and South Eastern European countries (Croatia, Estonia, Latvia, Lithuania, Serbia, and Slovenia) in PISA 2006. This chapter describes the participation rates by countries and the demographic characteristics of the students with special educational needs as a group, as well as by their disability status. Students' educational experiences and perceptions are presented as well as their perceptions of their learning behaviours. In general, too few students with special education needs are included in PISA from not enough economies and the conclusions that can be drawn are therefore extremely limited.

Introduction

International and national legislation, policies, and advocacy initiatives demand equity and social inclusion for students with disabilities in all aspects of school reforms, programmes and services. Standards-based reform demands that education systems set high academic content standards for all children and that they develop assessment and accountability systems to ensure that all children learn to very high levels. The expectation is that education systems will implement inclusive instruction and assessment programmes, assuring that all students, including students with special educational needs have the opportunity to participate in high quality instruction and learning activities that will lead to valued social and vocational outcomes.

While interest in the physical and academic inclusion of students with special educational needs in general education schools and classrooms has steadily increased across the world in the past two decades, their corresponding inclusion in standardised assessment and accountability systems has not proceeded at the same pace (OECD,2007).

---

[9] This chapter was prepared by Barbara LeRoy, Preethy Samuel and Peter Bahr from Wayne State University, with Peter Evans and Marcella Deluca

[10] Technical Note: This study is an exploratory, descriptive examination of the performance of students who reside in Baltic and South Eastern European countries and Malta and are identified as having special educational needs via the procedures used in PISA. For those variables in which only descriptive values were provided measures of standard error or standard deviation are not supplied. These measures are provided however for the scores obtained on the PISA tests. There are no assumptions that the findings in this paper are representative of the special education population in the selected countries. For all of these reasons, the results described are to be treated with caution and are in need of replication.

Numerous issues have contributed to the slow integration of these students into assessment systems, including concerns about participation options, test accommodations, alternate assessment formats, reporting results, and accountability (National Centre for Educational Outcomes-NCEO, October 2003). The educational programme of OECD has similarly been concerned with public accountability of education and the comparative functioning of education systems across the world, for all students. The OECD/PISA programme provides an international mechanism for examining the education systems and outcomes for secondary students with disabilities, difficulties, and disadvantages in their sample, thus allowing for the gathering and interpretation of access, performance, and outcome statistics for this population.

In 2005 LeRoy, Kulik, Tamassia, Evans and Deluca (OECD, 2007) conducted the first study related to students with special educational needs in PISA 2003. Findings focused on descriptions of participation by country and student demography, and performance by academic areas, learner behaviours, and social background. This study was replicated by the same authors in 2008 using PISA 2006 programme data. This current study uses the same research design, questions, and methodology to examine PISA 2006 participation and performance for students with special educational needs (SEN) who reside in Baltic and South Eastern European countries. Specifically, it describes the participation of students with special education needs from these countries in the OECD PISA 2006 programme, addressing participation by country and student demography. Performance is examined related to typical students, learner behaviours, and social background. The discussion presents the study's findings in relation to the PISA SEN population in general and the PISA OECD and European Union (EU) samples, specifically.

Background

Overview of the Programme for International Student Assessment (PISA)

PISA is a large scale, multinational OECD programme which is designed to develop internationally comparable indicators that inform the process of education policy, reinforce the public accountability of education, and provide insight into the comparative functioning of education systems. PISA provides basic, contextual, and trend indicators. PISA is different from most educational assessments because it examines young people's capacity to use their knowledge and skills in order to meet real life challenges, rather than merely looking for mastery of school curricula. The assessment uses multiple-choice and open-ended questions to assess academic knowledge and skills in the areas of reading, maths, science, problem-solving, and computer technology. In addition, information is gathered on the students' attitudes and approaches to learning, and student and school demographic backgrounds. New to the student demographic background in PISA 2003 was a distinct variable identifying the student's special education status.

The PISA assessment is implemented every three years, with a sample of 15 year-old students from each participating country. The inaugural 2000 PISA focused on reading literacy, and gathered data from 265 000 students from 32 countries. The 2003 assessment, which examined mathematics proficiency, included 274 524 students from 41 countries. All OECD member countries participated in PISA 2003, as well as 11 partner countries. The focus of PISA 2006 was science competencies. All OECD member countries participated in PISA 2006 and 27 partner countries. Data was gathered from nearly 400 000 students.

The sampling strategy for identifying eligible schools and students has strict guidelines regarding exclusions. At the school level, 0.5% of the population may be excluded due to geographic inaccessibility, and another 2.0% may be excluded due to the segregated nature of their population, *e.g.* schools that only serve students who meet the student exclusion criteria as stated below. Another 2.5% of the population may be excluded if the students are identified as either having a functional disability, an intellectual disability, or a limited proficiency in the test language.

Purpose of the study

This study examines the PISA 2006 participation and performance of students with special educational needs who reside in Baltic and South Eastern European countries. The study describes the participation rates by countries and the demographic characteristics of the students with special educational needs as a group, as well as by their disability status. Students' educational experiences and perceptions are presented as well as their perceptions of their learning behaviours. A major intent of this study is to examine the performance of students with special educational needs on PISA science, mathematics, and reading. This performance is compared to typical PISA participants for the three skill areas. The strength of the relationships between learner behaviours and science performance, and student Economic, Social and Cultural Status (ESCS) and science performance for students with special educational needs is explored. Furthermore, performance is examined by type of disability. Finally, student perceptions of their information and communication technology access and competence, as well as selected school characteristics for students with special needs are described. For comparative purposes, the results for the Baltic and South Eastern European SEN students are compared to SEN student samples from PISA, OECD, and the European Union on selected variables.

Study questions

Specifically, this study addressed the following primary questions:

1. What is the PISA 2006 participation rate of Baltic and South Eastern European students with special educational needs by country?
2. What are the demographic characteristics of the Baltic and South Eastern European students with special educational needs who participated in PISA 2006?
3. What were the educational experiences and perceptions of school of the Baltic and South Eastern European students with special educational needs who participated in PISA 2006?
4. How do Baltic and South Eastern European students with special educational needs perform on PISA 2006 (mathematics, reading, science competencies)?
5. How do Baltic and South Eastern European students with special educational needs compare to typical Baltic and South Eastern European PISA students in effective learner behaviours (attitudes toward science)?
6. What is the relationship between effective learner behaviours and PISA performance for Baltic and South Eastern European students with special educational needs?

7. How do Baltic and South Eastern European students with special educational needs compare to typical Baltic and South Eastern European PISA students on economic, social and cultural status (ESCS)?
8. What is the relationship between the ESCS backgrounds of Baltic and South Eastern European students with special educational needs and their PISA performance?
9. What were the perceptions of Baltic and South Eastern European students with special educational needs with regard to information and communication technology (ICT) access and competence?

Related to questions 1-4, 6 and 9 above the following secondary question was addressed: How does the Baltic and South Eastern European countries' SEN sample compare to the other SEN samples (*e.g.* PISA, OECD and EU)?

Methodology

Subjects

The subjects for this study were students with special educational needs from Baltic and South Eastern European countries who participated in PISA 2006. The specific Baltic and South Eastern European countries that were included in the study are Bulgaria, Croatia, Estonia, Latvia, Lithuania, Montenegro, Romania, Serbia, and Slovenia. The students with special educational needs were identified through the PISA Student Tracking Form under the code of SEN (special education needs). Within that code, students could be classified as one of five types: no special education needs; functional disability; intellectual disability; limited test language proficiency; and other. Functional disability was defined as having a moderate to severe permanent physical disability. Intellectual disability was defined as having a mental or emotional disability and having being either tested as cognitively delayed or is considered in the professional opinion of qualified staff to be cognitively delayed (PISA 2004). The last category, other, was uniquely defined by each country PISA manager and approved by the international PISA centre. No students from Baltic and South Eastern European countries were identified under the code of 'other'. For selected questions, the students with no special education needs (code 0) were used for comparative analyses. In addition, for comparative analyses among students with special educational needs, SEN samples from PISA, OECD, and the EU were used. The students who were included in the PISA database were identified as above; participated in the assessment; and the following data exist: demographics; background information; performance in mathematics, reading and science; all student questionnaire variables, and all school questionnaire variables.

Variables

Five sources of data were used to complete this study: the student tracking form; the student questionnaire; the student performance outcomes; the school questionnaire, and the ICT familiarity component of the student questionnaire. The datasets were merged using a distinct linking variable across the sets.

Limitations

The major limitations of this study include:

- The definitions of type of disability are very broad and do not match any specific national or international definitions or criteria such as the resource model of defining special education needs as presented by OECD (OECD, 2007).

- The sample sizes are very small and any inferential findings should be viewed with extreme caution.

- The small sample sizes also make international comparisons difficult.

- The SEN sample is unevenly distributed across the countries.

- No attempt was made to examine student performance by country, given the small overall size of the sample and the extremely small size of the subsamples within each country.

Findings

The findings from this descriptive study will be presented by the study questions.

- **Question 1: What is the PISA 2006 participation rate of Baltic and South Eastern European students with special educational needs by country?**

As shown in Table 7.1, nine Baltic and South Eastern European countries participated in PISA 2006. Out of those nine countries, six included a total of 292 students with special educational needs, representing .65% of the total PISA population for the region. By category, these special educational needs students included 52 students with functional disabilities (17.8%), 219 students with intellectual disabilities (75%) and 21 students with limited language proficiency (7.2%). There were no students identified as 'other' under their national programme managers' discretion. Among the Baltic and South Eastern European countries, only Bulgaria, Montenegro and Romania did not include students with special educational needs in their assessments.

Overall, Lithuania included the highest percentage of students with special educational needs in its sample, at 2.42% of its total participants. The remaining other five countries had less than one percent of their country samples composed of students with special educational needs. In both Estonia and Latvia, more than 10% of their special educational needs subsample were students with limited test language proficiency.

Table 7.1 **SEN Students by Baltic and South Eastern European country (n=292)**

Country	PISA Sample	SEN Students	% SEN in Sample	Functional Disability		Intellectual Disability		Limited Language Proficiency (LLP)	
				n	%	n	%	n	%
Bulgaria	4 498	0	0.00%	0	-	0	-	0	-
Croatia	5 213	40	0.77%	3	7.5%	35	87.5%	2	5.0%
Estonia	4 865	45	0.92%	7	15.6%	32	71.1%	6	13.3%
Latvia	4 719	27	0.57%	10	37.0%	13	48.2%	4	14.8%
Lithuania	4 744	115	2.42%	20	17.1%	90	78.3%	5	4.4%
Montenegro	4 455	0	0.00%	0	-	0	-	0	--
Romania	5 118	0	0.00%	0	-	0	-	0	--
Serbia	4 798	5	0.10%	3	60.0%	2	40.0%	0	--
Slovenia	6 595	60	0.91%	9	15.0%	47	78.3%	4	6.7%
Total	**45 005**	**292**	**0.65%**	**52**	**17.8%**	**219**	**75.0%**	**21**	**7.20%**

- **Question 2: What are the demographic characteristics of the Baltic and South Eastern European students with special educational needs who participated in PISA 2006?**
- **Question 2a: How do the demographic characteristics of the Baltic and South Eastern European students with special educational needs compare to those of PISA, OECD, and EU SEN samples?**

Table 7.2 presents the demographic characteristics of the Baltic and South Eastern European students who participated in PISA 2006. Typical students were nearly evenly divided by gender, while the majority of students with special educational needs were male. The majority of the typical students were in grades 9 and 10 (lower secondary), while students with special educational needs were spread across grades 8–10. Overall, the majority of parents of typical and SEN students completed upper secondary and post-secondary education. However, parents of typical students had slightly higher educational attainment than parents of SEN students. Mothers of SEN students were less likely to have attained higher levels of education than all other parents. A higher percentage of parents of typical students had white collar jobs as compared to parents of SEN students. Furthermore, with regard to occupational status, the modal response for parents of typical students was white collar, high skilled occupation. While the modal response for a parent of SEN students was blue collar, high skilled occupation.

Table 7.2 **Demographic characteristics of Baltic and South Eastern European students in PISA 2006**

Characteristic	Not SEN		SEN	
Disability	n	%	n	%
Functional	n/a	n/a	52	17.8%
Intellectual	n/a	n/a	219	75.0%
LLP	n/a	n/a	21	7.2%
Gender	n	%	n	%
Male	22 894	51.2	188	64.4
Female	21 819	48.8	104	35.6
Current Grade	n	%	n	%
7th grade	258	0.6	25	0.1
8th grade	2 864	6.4	75	25.7
9th grade	31 617	70.8	126	43.2
10th grade	9 593	21.5	64	21.9
11th grade	329	0.7	0	0

Parent Education	Mother		Father		Mother		Father	
	n	%	n	%	n	%	n	%
None	133	0.3	119	0.3	6	2.2	4	1.6
ISCED 1/Primary	446	1.0	460	1.0	4	1.5	7	2.8
ISCED 2/Lower Secondary	5 456	12.7	4241	9.5	63	23.6	41	16.3
ISCED 3/Upper Secondary	17 153	39.8	19433	43.5	81	30.3	99	39.4
ISCED 4, 5, 6/Post Secondary, Tertiary	19 930	46.2	17326	38.7	113	42.3	100	39.8

Highest Parent Occupational Status	n	%	n	%
White collar high skilled	20 089		44.9	77	28.6
White collar low skilled	10 388		24.5	66	24.5
Blue collar high skilled	7 375		17.4	85	31.6
Blue collar low skilled	4 620		10.9	41	15.2

Table 7.3 presents the demographic characteristics of the Baltic and South Eastern European SEN students by SEN category. The largest single group of students had intellectual disabilities, followed by students with functional disabilities, and students with limited test language proficiency, respectively. The majority of all students, independent of the presence or not of a disability were in grade 9. The mean age of the students was 15.8 years. There was no difference in mean age by the presence of a disability. Similar percentages of parents had post-secondary education (ISCED 4 and above), except for parents of students with intellectual disabilities. Consistent with

educational attainment, the parents with the highest levels of education had white collar, high skilled occupations.

Table 7.3 **Demographic characteristics of Baltic and South Eastern European SEN students in PISA 2006 by type of disability (n=292)**

Characteristic	Not SEN	Functional Disability	Intellectual Disability	Limited Language Proficiency
Gender	N=44713	N=52	N=219	N=21
Male	51.2	67.3	63.9	61.9
Female	48.8	32.7	36.1	38.1
Current Grade				
7th grade	0.6	5.8	9.7	4.8
8th grade	6.4	21.2	27.6	19.0
9th grade	70.8	50.0	40.6	57.1
10th grade	21.5	23.1	22.1	19.0
11th grade	0.7	0.0.	0.0	0.0
Education – Mother				
None	0.3	0.0	3.0	0.0
ISCED 1	1.0	0.0	2.0	0.0
ISCED 2	12.7	22.4	23.2	30.0
ISCED 3	39.8	26.5	32.3	20.0
ISCED 4, 5, 6	46.2	51.0	39.4	50.0
Education – Father				
None	0.3	0.0	2.2	0.0
ISCED 1	1.1	0.0	3.8	0.0
ISCED 2	10.2	13.0	16.7	21.1
ISCED 3	46.7	41.3	39.8	31.6
ISCED 4, 5, 6	41.7	45.7	37.6	47.4
Highest Parent Occupational Status				
White collar high skilled	47.3	41.2	24.1	42.1
White collar low skilled	24.5	21.6	26.6	10.5
Blue collar high skilled	17.4	23.5	32.7	42.1
Blue collar low skilled	10.9	13.7	16.6	5.3

Table 7.3a **Demographic characteristics of SEN students by sample**

Characteristic	PISA					OECD					EU					Baltic & SE Countries				
	A	B	C	D	E	A	B	C	D	E	A	B	C	D	E	A	B	C	D	E
Gender (% Male)	49	49	49	54	48	50	55	65	52	72	50	54	64	52	72	51	67	64	62	0
Grade (% Upper Secondary)	86	79	77	85	94	85	75	68	74	89	85	69	61	72	89	91	73	63	76	0
Mother's Education (% Post Secondary)	48	48	54	51	58	31	31	29	24	35	33	30	25	23	35	46	51	39	50	0
Father's Education (% Post Secondary)	46	44	49	50	50	31	26	27	29	26	30	26	23	26	26	42	46	38	47	0
Parent Occupation (% White Collar)	51	52	56	60	43	53	50	37	36	50	51	48	32	31	50	47	41	24	42	0

Codes: A: No Disability; B: Functional Disability; C: Intellectual Disability; D: Limited Test Language Proficiency and E: Other, as designated by the National Programme Manager

Table 7.3a presents the demographic characteristics of SEN students by PISA, OECD, and EU samples. In terms of the demographic characteristics of the SEN students in this region, the students were similar to SEN students who participated in PISA and EU SEN students in terms of disability prevalence in the sample, age, and grade level (ISCED) in school. With regard to gender, the Baltic and Eastern European sample of SEN students were predominately male, while gender was equally divided in the PISA sample. The Baltic and Eastern European student gender split more closely paralleled international ratios (*e.g.* two-thirds male). Additionally, parents of SEN students in PISA, generally, and within the EU sample tended to be slightly more educated (particularly mothers) and were more likely to have white collar, high skill occupations than those in the Baltic and Eastern European sample.

- **Question 3: What were the educational experiences and perceptions of school of the Baltic and South Eastern European students with special educational needs who participated in PISA 2006?**
- **Question 3a: How do the educational experiences and perceptions of school of the Baltic and South Eastern European students with special educational needs compare to those of PISA, OECD, and EU SEN samples?**

Table 7.4 presents the educational experiences and perceptions of school of the SEN students. For this set of variables, the SEN group data was aggregated as the overall response rate was only 10% of the SEN sample. All SEN students and 99% of typical students attended public schools. The most frequently reported class size for typical students was 26-30 students per class. Students with special educational needs reported bimodal class sizes, either less than 15 or 26-30 students per class.

Ability grouping was examined both for in class and out of class formats. For typical students, ability group both outside of the classroom and within the classroom occurred less than half of the time. Just over one-half of students with special educational needs reported no ability grouping outside of the classroom. With regard to classroom based ability grouping, the students reported more diversity, with some grouping by subjects being most common. The vast majority of all students reported that vocational training was not offered by their schools.

More than half of all students, independent of disability, participated in out of school tutoring. In terms of time spent studying, typical students reported that they spent between 2-4 hours per week on their lessons, while students with disabilities reported that they spent less than two hours per week on lessons. All students reported that they spent less than two hours per week on other homework assignments.

Table 7.4 **Baltic and South Eastern European SEN Students' Educational Experiences and Perceptions**

Perceptions of students	Not SEN	SEN
Attend public school (%)	99	100%
Class Size (%)		
<15 students	9.3	28.6
16-20 students	9.8	14.3
21-25 students	23.4	21.4
26-30 students	39.9	28.6
>31 students	17.7	7.1
Ability grouping outside class (%)		
All subjects	13.2	18.1
Some subjects	15.8	27.3
No subjects	71.0	54.6
Ability grouping inside class (%)		
All subjects	9.7	28.0
Some subjects	26.8	40.0
No subjects	53.5	32.0
Vocational Training (%)		
Not offered	72.5	85.8
<50% of time	13.4	7.1
> 50% of time	14.1	7.1
Participate in tutoring (%)	**50.9**	**55.4**
Time spent studying (hrs/ wk)		
Regular lessons	2-4	< 2
Homework	<2	<2

Table 7.4a presents the educational experiences and perceptions of school of SEN students by PISA, OECD, and EU samples. Unlike their counterparts in the larger PISA sample and the EU sample, all students in this region attended public schools. They also were educated in slightly larger classes than their counterparts. For typical students from this region, ability grouping was much less common than in the EU. SEN students in the region reported similar grouping patterns as in the larger sample and in the EU. While the opportunity for vocational training was low across all students and all PISA countries, the opportunity was negligible to non-existent in the Baltic and Eastern European countries. However, these generalisations should be observed with caution as the response rates were very low on some of the questions for the SEN students. Finally, all Baltic and Eastern European students reported that they participated in tutoring twice as often as students in the PISA population. On the other hand, the tutoring rate was consistent with responses from EU students. Studying behaviour was similar across all groups and samples.

Table 7.4a **SEN Students' educational experiences and perceptions by sample**

Experience/ Perception	PISA					OECD					EU					Baltic & SE Countries	
	A	B	C	D	E	A	B	C	D	E	A	B	C	D	E	A	SEN*
Attend Public School (%)	83	99	85	78	87	83	89	80	81	84	82	89	79	27	84	99	100
Class Size (%)																	
<15 Students	7	29	42	30	14	4	9	25	15	2	5	14	29	18	2	9	29
16-20 Students	13	0	20	35	14	15	14	22	29	15	17	13	23	26	15	10	14
21-25 Students	24	29	23	20	32	32	38	33	35	39	39	44	28	38	39	23	21
26-30 Students	23	36	36	11	13	25	30	18	15	38	28	25	18	11	38	40	29
>31 Students	33	6	4	2	4	23	8	2	5	5	12	4	3	6	5	18	7
Ability Grouping Outside Class (%)																	
All Subjects	13	18	9	12	0	10	12	9	12	2	10	18	10	13	2	13	18
Some Subjects	33	27	39	32	12	41	41	49	39	27	28	25	39	27	27	16	27
No Subjects	54	55	52	56	88	49	47	42	49	71	62	57	51	60	71	71	55
Ability Grouping Within Class (%)																	
All Subjects	12	36	16	2	0	9	6	8	6	0	6	7	9	9	0	9	28
Some Subjects	42	46	48	64	58	45	50	51	47	48	42	51	47	39	48	27	40
No Subjects	46	18	36	34	42	46	44	41	47	52	52	43	44	52	52	54	32
Vocational Training (%)																	
None	72	69	53	57	89	69	61	42	58	94	69	70	43	59	94	73	86
<50% time	13	23	12	13	0	14	17	17	14	1	8	7	12	7	1	13	7
>50% time	15	8	35	30	11	17	22	41	28	5	23	23	45	34	5	14	7
Participate in Tutoring (%)	23	23	19	20	25	46	55	57	66	65	52	63	61	70	65	51	55
Time Spent Studying (hrs/week)																	
Regular Lessons	4	4	4	4	4	4	3	3	3	3	3	3	3	3	3	3	1
Homework	2	2	2	2	2	2	2	1	2	2	2	2	1	2	2	1	1

Codes: A: No Disability; B: Functional Disability; C: Intellectual Disability; D: Limited Test Language Proficiency, and E: Other, as designated by the National Programme Manager

- **Question 4: How do Baltic and South Eastern European students with special educational needs perform on PISA 2006 (mathematics, reading, and science competencies)?**
- **Question 4a: How does the performance of the Baltic and South Eastern European students with special educational needs compare to that of PISA, OECD, and EU SEN samples?**

The focus of PISA 2006 was science literacy. Scientific literacy is defined in terms of an individual's:

- Scientific knowledge and use of that knowledge to identify questions, to acquire new knowledge, to explain scientific phenomena, and to draw evidence-based conclusions about science-related issues
- Understanding of the characteristic features of science as a form of human knowledge and enquiry
- Awareness of how science and technology shape our material, intellectual and cultural environments
- Willingness to engage with science-related issues and with the ideas of science, as a reflective citizen (OECD, 2007, p. 34-35).

Each student is given a score based on the difficulty of tasks that he/she could reliably perform. The average student score is 500. Student performance scores are also divided into six proficiency levels, with Level 6 representing the highest scores (and hence the most difficult tasks) and Level 1 the lowest scores (and hence the easiest tasks). Proficiency relates to a student's capacity to analyse, reason and communicate effectively when using science. Brief summaries of typical student skills by proficiency level are described below.

Level 1: Students have such a limited scientific knowledge that it can only be applied to a few, familiar situations. They can present scientific explanations that are obvious and that follow explicitly from given evidence.

Level 2: Students have adequate scientific knowledge to provide possible explanations in familiar contests or draw conclusions based on simple investigations. They are capable of direct reasoning and making literal interpretations of the results of scientific inquiry or technological problem solving.

Level 3: Students can identify clearly described scientific issues in a range of contexts. They can select facts and knowledge to explain phenomena and apply simple models or inquiry strategies. Students can interpret and use scientific concepts from different disciplines and can apply them directly. They can develop short statements using facts and make decisions based on scientific knowledge.

Level 4: Students can work effectively with situations and issues that may involve explicit phenomena requiring them to make inferences about eh role of science or technology. They can select and integrate explanations from different disciplines of science or technology and link those explanations directly to aspects of life situations. Students can reflect on their actions and they can communicate decisions using scientific knowledge and evidence.

Level 5: Students can identify the scientific components of many complex life situations, apply both scientific concepts and knowledge about science to those situations and can compare, select and evaluate appropriate scientific evidence for responding to life situations. Students can use well-developed inquiry abilities, link knowledge appropriately and bring critical insights to situations. They can construct explanations based on evidence and arguments based on their critical analysis.

Level 6: Students can consistently identify, explain and apply scientific knowledge and knowledge about science in a variety of complex life situations. They can link different information sources and explanations and use evidence from those sources to justify decisions. They clearly and consistently demonstrate advanced scientific thinking and reasoning, and they demonstrate willingness to use their scientific understanding in support of solutions to unfamiliar scientific and technological situations. Students can use scientific knowledge and develop arguments in support of recommendations and decisions that centre on personal, social or global situations (OECD, 2007, p. 43).

While not being the focus of PISA 2006, students also completed test items in reading and mathematics, which were scored using the same proficiency scale format.

Table 7.5 presents the mean performance scores using the standard test format for mathematics, reading, and science by type of student. Overall, students with disabilities and students with limited test language proficiency scored lower than typical students in each academic area. Within disability, students with functional disabilities scored higher than students with intellectual disabilities. They also scored higher than students with limited test language proficiency in mathematics and science, but not in reading.

Table 7.5 **Comparisons of Baltic and South Eastern European SEN student performance on PISA 2006**

Area/ Disability	*n*	Mean	SD	SE/Mean
Math				
None	44 713	439.22	94.04	2.16
Functional Disability	52	409.31	103.15	22.43
Intellectual Disability	219	342.19	79.00	6.89
Limited Language Proficiency	21	407.68	76.25	26.43
Reading				
None	44 713	423.29	102.71	2.27
Functional Disability	52	399.12	99.04	19.99
Intellectual Disability	219	323.51	92.24	7.96
Limited Language Proficiency	21	402.50	90.74	25.27
Science				
None	44 713	447.36	94.56	2.01
Functional Disability	52	424.52	93.79	17.90
Intellectual Disability	219	355.32	75.99	6.79
Limited Language Proficiency	21	407.77	82.85	26.34

Table 7.5a presents the academic performance of SEN students by PISA, OECD, and EU samples. In terms of academic performance across all three areas, mathematics, reading, and science, students from the Baltic and South Eastern European Countries

scored lower than the SEN students in the other samples, with the exception of students with limited test language proficiency. The scores, overall, were driven by Estonia and Slovenia as their mean scores were significantly above the OECD average (mean scores – science scale: Estonia: 531, Slovenia: 519). Students with functional disabilities and those with intellectual disabilities scored considerably lower than their counterparts in the other samples. In terms of science performance specifically, the mean scores for Baltic and South Eastern European students with SEN were on par with the bottom one quarter of the country rankings, indicating that the scores were significantly below OECD averages for PISA 2006. Finally, only those students with limited test language proficiency from the region scored higher than their counterparts in the rest of the world. These same students also reported the highest use of computers and technology which may contribute to their relatively high performance scores, particularly in science.

Table 7.5a **SEN student performance on PISA 2006 by sample**

Sample		Math		Reading		Science	
	n	MN	SE	MN	SE	MN	SE
PISA							
None	394 290	455	(1)	447	(1)	462	(1)
FD	421	427	(10)	428	(13)	435	(13)
ID	1 906	409	(5)	375	(8)	408	(6)
LLP	877	405	17	355	13	396	15
Other	426	495	(7)	490	(9)	497	(7)
OECD							
None	247 519	485	(1)	486	(1)	492	(1)
FD	314	438	(11)	450	(13)	448	(15)
ID	1 605	413	(5)	383	(8)	411	(6)
LLP	801	406	(15)	376	(8)	394	(12)
Other	426	495	(7)	490	(9)	497	(7)
EU							
None	163 468	492	(1)	487	(1)	500	(1)
FD	254	456	(12)	459	(14)	466	(13)
ID	1 331	405	(6)	384	(7)	408	(6)
LLP	544	382	(8)	366	(8)	380	(9)
Other	426	495	(7)	490	(9)	497	(7)
Baltic + SEE Countries							
None	44 713	439	(2)	423	(2)	447	(2)
FD	439	409	(22)	399	(20)	425	(18)
ID	94	342	(7)	324	(8)	355	(7)
LLP	2	408	(26)	403	(25)	408	(26)
Other	--	--		--		--	

Figures 7.1-7.3 depict the mean performance by proficiency level of students with special educational needs as compared to typical PISA 2006 participants on mathematics, reading, and science, respectively. As can be seen, the vast majority of students with special educational needs fell below the midpoint (Level 3) in all performance areas. The modal response in mathematics was at Level 2 for typical students, below Level 1 for students with functional and intellectual disabilities, and at Level 1 for students with limited test language proficiency. The modal response in reading was below Level 1 for all students. For science, the modal response for typical students and students with limited test language proficiency was at Level 2, while students with functional or intellectual disabilities had a modal response below Level 1. Across all academic areas, the majority of students with intellectual disabilities scored below level one in proficiency.

Figure 7.1 **Comparison of student mathematics proficiency by SEN**

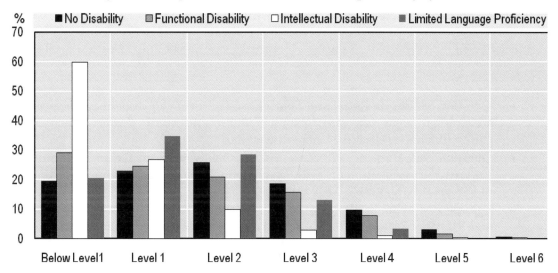

Figure 7.2 **Comparison of student reading proficiency by SEN**

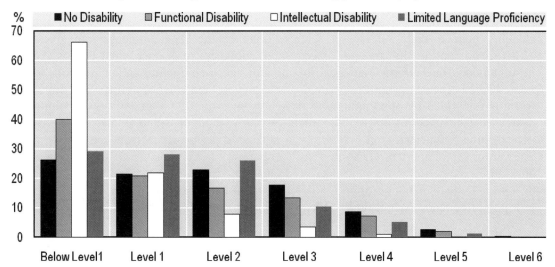

Figure 7.3 **Comparison of student science proficiency by SEN**

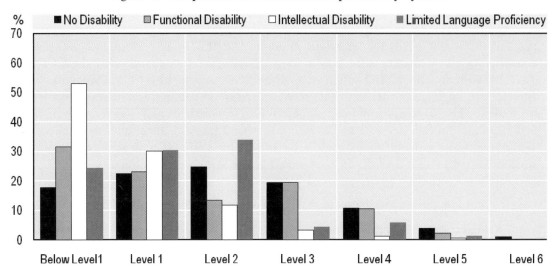

- **Question 5: How do Baltic and South Eastern European students with special educational needs compare to typical Baltic and South Eastern European PISA students on effective learner behaviours?**
- **Question 5a: How do effective learner behaviours of Baltic and South Eastern European students with special educational needs compare to those of PISA, OECD, and EU SEN samples?**
- **Question 6: What is the relationship between effective learner behaviours and PISA performance for Baltic and South Eastern European students with special educational needs?**

PISA 2006 assessed students' beliefs and behaviours toward learning science, under the assumption that student performance is impacted by their beliefs and behaviours. PISA identifies four characteristics of effective learners: Beliefs about the importance of academic performance; motivation; attributions for performance; and opportunities for self-directed learning. Beliefs about academic performance examine how important students believe their efforts in science, mathematics and language are overall. Motivation is defined by students' interest and enjoyment of science; their beliefs about its importance in their personal goal attainment; and their feelings about school. Self-related beliefs focus on confidence and self-efficacy in their science ability. Self-directed learning is defined by opportunities to design science questions, express own opinions, design science experiments, choose their own investigations, and conduct their own investigations. Statements on beliefs about academic performance were measured on a scale from very important (1) to not at all important (4). Statements on motivation and attributions for performance were measured on a scale from strongly agree (1) to strongly disagree (4). Statements on opportunities for self-directed learning were measured on a four point frequency scale from in all lessons (1) to never or hardly at all (4).

Table 7.6 presents the means of Baltic and South Eastern European students with special educational needs on the four aspects of effective learner behaviours, as compared to typical PISA participants from the same region. Across all learner behaviours, students with intellectual disabilities had lower scores than typical students or other students with learning needs. Overall, students, with and without disabilities, felt strongly that academic performance across all subjects was important, with the exception of students with intellectual disabilities. Slightly more than half of them agreed with the belief. More than 90% of students with limited test language proficiency believed that it was important to do well in academics. In terms of motivation, approximately two-thirds of the students were positively motivated to learn science. Again the exception to this finding was students with intellectual disabilities. Just over half of them expressed motivation to learn science. All students were only moderately confident in their science abilities. Finally, related to self-directed learning in their classrooms, students with functional disabilities and those with limited test language proficiency reported more opportunities than the typical students or students with intellectual disabilities. Typical students reported that they had the least number of opportunities for self directed learning.

Table 7.6 **Beliefs and behaviours of South Eastern European SEN students toward learning**

	Without SEN (%)	**SEN (%)**		
Belief/Behaviour		*FD*	*ID*	*LLP*
Believe it is important to do well in academics	78.9	78.2	61.8	90.5
Well motivated to learn science	67.9	72.1	56.2	64.3
Believe that they will do well in science classes	58.6	57.9	43.1	60.5
Report opportunities for self-directed learning	28.1	46.1	31.4	43.8

Table 7.6a presents the beliefs and behaviours of SEN students toward learning by sample. In general, students from this region thought that academic performance was less important than their counterparts in the EU or PISA, with the exception of students with limited test language proficiency. These regional students rated the importance of academic performance higher than their counterparts. Motivation and self confidence ratings were similar to EU and PISA ratings. While students from the Baltic and South Eastern European regions reported more opportunities for self-directed learning, the low number of responses to this variable makes generalizations impossible.

Table 7.6a **Beliefs and behaviours of SEN students toward learning by sample**

Belief/ Behaviour	PISA					OECD					EU					Baltic & SE Countries			
	A	B	C	D	E	A	B	C	D	E	A	B	C	D	E	A	B	C	D
Academic Performance Valued (% Yes)	86	86	85	84	84	86	84	80	84	83	84	84	81	84	83	79	78	62	91
Motivation in Science	69	66	63	61	70	65	65	61	68	68	64	68	62	69	68	68	72	56	64
Self-efficacy in Science	61	57	56	57	59	58	57	51	56	56	57	58	52	56	56	59	58	43	61
Self-directed learning in Science	31	28	24	26	25	27	32	34	38	28	24	34	34	39	28	28	46	31	44

Codes: A: No Disability; B: Functional Disability; C: Intellectual disability; D: Limited test language proficiency; E: Other, as designated by the National Programme Manager

Table 7.7 presents the relationship between learner beliefs and behaviours and performance. For typical students each of the four beliefs and behaviours were significantly correlated with their performance. For students with functional disabilities and students with intellectual disabilities there was a positive correlation between reported opportunities for self-directed learning and performance. As opportunities for self directed learning increased, so, too, did performance. There were no significant correlations between beliefs/behaviours and performance for students with limited test language proficiency. However, the sample size was extremely small.

Table 7.7 **Effects of beliefs and behaviours on Baltic and South Eastern European SEN student performance**

Beliefs	Without SEN			Functional Disability			Intellectual Disability			Limited Language Proficiency		
	Mean	SD	r	Mean	SD	r	Mean	SD	r	Mean	SD	r
Believe it is important to do well in academics	1.77	0.55	-0.09**	1.79	0.53	0.13	1.84	0.71	0.03	1.62	0.46	0.16
Well motivated to learn science	2.14	0.67	0.04**	1.93	0.69	0.21	2.11	0.72	0.07	2.2	0.67	0.37
Believe that they will do well in science classes	2.31	0.55	-0.01	2.26	0.55	0.17	2.37	0.62	0.06	2.32	0.45	-0.01
Report opportunity for self-directed learning	2.96	0.65	0.32**	2.6	0.85	0.43**	2.66	0.79	0.32**	2.64	0.67	0.41
Science	Mn/SD			469.22/93.61			436.44/87.54			366.54/74.97		

**$p<0.01$

- **Question 7: How do Baltic and South Eastern European students with special educational needs compare to typical Baltic and South Eastern European PISA students on economic, social and cultural status (ESCS)?**

PISA created the index of economic, social and cultural status (ESCS) to capture aspects of a student's family, home background and occupational status. ESCS is derived from the following indices: the highest international socio-economic index of occupational status of the father or mother (HISEI); the highest level of education of the father or mother (HISCED); the number of cultural possessions at home (CULTPOSS), other possessions in the home (HOPOS-WEALTH) and home educational resources (HEDRES) (Questions 13-15 on the Student Questionnaire) (OECD, 2006). The rationale for this set of variables is that socio-economic status is usually determined by a combination of occupational status, education, and wealth. Access to relevant household items is used as a proxy for wealth, since there is no direct variable in the PISA database for family income. The indices are standardized so that the mean of the index value for the OECD student population is zero with a standard deviation of one. A negative value on the index indicates that the students answered less positively than all students did on average across OECD countries. Similarly, a positive value on an index indicates that the students answered more favourably, or more positively, than students did, on average, in OECD countries (OECD, 2007, p. 332).

Table 7.8 presents the ESCS characteristics of Baltic and South Eastern European students with special educational needs by type of disability. All students, independent of the presence of a disability, indicated a less positive response to the economic, social and cultural variables than did all students across OECD countries. Within the sample, typical students and students with intellectual disabilities were least positive about their ESC status.

Table7.8 **ESCS characteristics of Baltic and South Eastern European SEN students**

ESCS indices	No SEN	SEN (means)		
		FD	ID	LLP
Cultural possessions at home (-1.79 to 1.46)	0.23	0.05	-0.31	-0.05
Index of home possessions (-6.54 to 4.44)	-0.22	-0.2	-0.71	-0.15
Home educational resources (-4.60 to 1.41)	-0.16	-0.07	-0.62	-0.13
Family wealth (-3.85 to 3.29)	-0.53	-0.52	-0.76	-0.44
Index of economic, social and cultural status (-4.64 to 3.12)	-0.55	-0.17	-0.59	-0.23

- **Question 8: What is the relationship between the ESCS backgrounds of Baltic and South Eastern European students with special educational needs and their PISA performance?**

Table 7.9 compares overall student performance on mathematics, reading, and science by ESCS level (highest one-third versus lowest one-third). Across all performance areas, students with the highest ESCS levels performed significantly higher than students from the lowest ESCS levels.

Table 7.9 **Comparison of Baltic and South Eastern European student performance by ESCS**

Subject	Highest 1/3 ESCS	Lowest 1/3 ESCS
Math (mean/ SD) r=0.40**	496.47/ 88.4	415.45/ 83.11
Below Level 1	7.69	31.94
Level 1	15.20	28.33
Level 2	24.35	23.69
Level 3	25.94	11.41
Level 4	17.83	3.78
Level 5	7.14	0.73
Level 6	1.83	0.09
Reading (mean/ SD) r=0.37**	483.02/ 93.48	402.65/ 93.84
Below Level 1	13.08	39.38
Level 1	16.25	24.83
Level 2	23.2	20.67
Level 3	25.09	10.98
Level 4	15.58	3.35
Level 5	5.67	0.72
Level 6	1.08	0.04
Science (mean/ SD) r=0.39**	507.14/ 91.73	425.96/ 85.3
Below Level 1	7.10	29.57
Level 1	14.47	28.68
Level 2	22.71	22.94
Level 3	25.71	12.78
Level 4	18.73	4.77
Level 5	8.63	1.05
Level 6	2.61	0.17

**p<0.001

Table 7.10 compares science performance by ESCS for Baltic and South Eastern European students with special educational needs. With the exception of students with functional disabilities, there was a significant relationship between ESCS level and science performance. Students with higher ESCS performed significantly higher in science than did students with lower ESCS. For students with functional disabilities, the finding was in the same direction as for the other groups, however the correlation was not statistically significant.

Table 7.10 **Comparison of Baltic and South Eastern European SEN student performance on PISA science by ESCS**

SEN category	*Highest 1/3 ESCS*	*Lowest 1/3 ESCS*
No SEN (mean/ SD) r=0.39**	507.5/ 91.48	426.64/ 85.24
Below Level 1 (%)	7.03%	29.43
Level 1	14.46	28.66
Level 2	22.74	23.011
Level 3	25.74	12.85
Level 4	18.76	4.80
Level 5	8.64	1.06
Level 6	2.62	0.18
Functional Disability (mean/ SD) r=0.09	441.1/ 94.19	418.71/ 67.48
Below Level 1	38.35	41.44
Level 1	4.91	30.78
Level 2	11.98	21.94
Level 3	30.25	5.85
Level 4	10.42	0
Level 5	4.09	0
Level 6	0	0
Intellectual Disability (mean/ SD) r=0.28**	385.74/ 106.31	349.1/ 55.49
Below Level 1	46.08	57.3
Level 1	29.46	32.83
Level 2	10.07	8.88
Level 3	6.07	0.99
Level 4	4.98	0
Level 5	3.34	0
Level 6	0	0
LLP (mean/ SD) r=.54**	466.46/ 81.92	401.62/ 80.2
Below Level 1	10.02	41.72
Level 1	21.19	37.95
Level 2	37.66	13.83
Level 3	8.58	4.58
Level 4	18.04	1.92
Level 5	4.51	0
Level 6	0	0

- **Question 9: What were the perceptions of Baltic and South Eastern European students with special educational needs with regard to information and communication technology (ICT) access and competence?**
- **Question 9a: How do the ICT access and competence perceptions of Baltic and South Eastern European students with special educational needs compare to those of PISA, OECD, and EU SEN samples?**

Students in 39 countries completed an optional PISA questionnaire (ICT) providing information about where students have access to computers, how often they use them and for what purposes. Specifically, the ICT was administered in Australia, Austria, Belgium, Canada, the Czech Republic, Denmark, Finland, Greece, Hungary, Iceland, Ireland, Italy, Japan, the Netherlands, New Zealand, Norway, Poland, Portugal, Korea, the Slovak Republic, Spain, Sweden, Switzerland, and Turkey, as well as the partner countries of Bulgaria, Chile, Colombia, Croatia, Jordan, Latvia, Macao-China, Montenegro, Qatar, the Russian Federation, Serbia, Slovenia, Thailand and Uruguay (OECD, 2007, p. 28). More than three thousands students with SEN had the opportunity to respond to the ICT questionnaire (n=3 151 or 77.1% of the student SEN sample). Responses to the item questionnaire were aggregated into four indices: ICT Internet/entertainment use (positive values on this index indicate high frequencies of ICT use); ICT programme/software use (positive values on this index indicate high frequencies of ICT use); Self confidence in ICT internet tasks (positive values on this index indicate high self confidence); and Self confidence in ICT high-level tasks (positive values on this index indicate high self confidence) (OECD, 2007, p. 342).

Specific to Baltic and South Eastern Europe, students in six of the nine countries in this study had the opportunity to complete the ICT questionnaire. As noted above the countries were Bulgaria, Croatia, Latvia, Montenegro, Serbia, and Slovenia. A total of 24 621 students completed the survey, including 123 SEN students (42% of the Baltic and South Eastern European SEN sample). Table 7.11 presents ICT access and perceptions of competence by type of student. All students reported extremely high use of information and communication technology for internet and entertainment use. The score on this index was primarily driven by question 1 – 'have you ever used a computer?', in which more than 93% of all students responded positively. Less than half of all the students reported that they have been using computers for more than five years. Students with intellectual disabilities and those with limited test language proficiency were least likely to have had long term access to computers and technology.

More than half of all the students reported that they use a computer at home on a daily basis. By contrast, less than 10% of typical students and students with functional disabilities reported that they used computers at school on a daily basis. No students with limited test language proficiency reported that they use computers on a daily basis at school. Students with intellectual disabilities reported the most use of computers on a daily basis at school. In terms of activities, students reported that they used computers must often to play games, download software, and communicate with others, respectively.

In terms of using programmes and software on a daily basis, less than half of all students reported daily use of any types of programmes and software, with the exception of students with limited test language proficiency. Sixty percent of them reported daily use of computer programmes. Generally speaking, students were most likely to use graphics and computer programmes versus spreadsheets, educational software and word processing software.

With regard to self confidence in the use of information and communication technology to perform internet tasks, there was variability among the student groups and within tasks. In terms of group variability, students with intellectual disabilities were least likely to express self-confidence across the internet tasks, while students with limited test language proficiency were most likely to express self-confidence, followed by typical students. In terms of tasks, all students reported above average confidence in three tasks: chatting on-line; downloading music; and sending emails. Students were moderately confident in downloading files and searching for information. They were least confident in attaching files.

With regard to self confidence in the use of information and communication technology to perform high level tasks, three of the four student groups expressed moderate self confidence across all tasks. Students with intellectual disabilities were least confident across all tasks. In terms of specific tasks, students were moderately confident with regard to controlling viruses, constructing websites, copying data, editing photos, and using spreadsheets, respectively. By contrast, less than half of the students expressed confidence in their ability to create databases, use word processing, move files, create presentations, and create multimedia presentations, in that order.

Table 7.11 **Information and Communication Technology (ICT) and SEN students**

ICT Items & Indices		SEN Type		
% Yes	**No SEN**	**FD**	**ID**	**LTLP**
Ever use computer	98.3	95.3	93.1	100
Use computer >5 years	36.3	48.8	20.8	26.7
Use at home daily	71.9	82.9	55.9	73.3
At school daily	5	7.3	19.7	0
At other places daily	8.6	7.1	18.5	6.7
Internet/Entertainment Use (% Daily)				
Browse	22.1	35.7	30.5	26.7
Games	36.3	38.1	42	40
Collaborate with group	14.1	14.3	23.4	33.3
Download software	30.1	26.2	30.7	40
Download music	9.1	9.5	19.4	20
Communication	30.5	28.6	31.7	26.7
Programme/Software Use (% Daily)				
Write documents	18.1	16.7	25.7	26.7
Spreadsheets	8.4	11.9	18.6	26.7
Graphics	43.3	40.5	36.1	40
Educational Software	10.9	16.7	21.8	26.7
Computer Programmes	46.8	26.8	32.4	60
Self-confidence-Internet tasks (% Well by myself)				
Chat on-line	79.9	73.8	55.6	93.3
Search for information	42.2	53.7	33.3	64.3
Download files	54.2	51.2	41	53.3
Attach Files	28.2	26.8	19.4	33.3
Download music	78.5	75.6	54.9	73.3
Send emails	82.1	73.2	53.1	66.7
Self-confidence high level tasks (% Well by myself)				
Control Viruses	85	87.8	65.5	73.3
Edit photos	71.5	68.3	41	80
Create databases	61.5	56.1	31.7	53.3
Copy data	75.5	70.7	47.1	86.7
Move Files	58.3	58.5	42.8	33.3
Use Word Processing	50.6	56.1	31.0	60.0
Use spreadsheets	73.9	73.2	55.9	60.0
Create presentations	37.9	48.8	35.7	60.0
Construct website	75.0	70.7	55.0	86.7
Create multimedia presentation	21.6	24.4	28.8	46.7

Table 7.11a presents the ICT perceptions of SEN students by PISA, OECD, and EU samples. As in the rest of the world, the vast majority of students in the Baltic and South Eastern European Countries has used computers and use them on a daily basis. However, compared to EU students and other PISA participants, students from this region have not been using computers on a regular basis as long. Additionally, these students reported

very low use of computers in school compared to the other PISA participants. As a general rule, the responses from SEN students from this region were similar to the SEN student responses from the other 39 countries who participated in the survey. In both instances, SEN students reported lower use and abilities than students without special educational needs.

With regard to use of computers, the responses from the Baltic and South Eastern European students were similar to their PISA counterparts. They are using them primarily for entertainment and communication with others. Likewise, they expressed similar levels of confidence and felt most skilled in chatting on-line, sending emails and downloading music. In addition, these students were similar to their peers in terms of self-confidence in performing high level tasks. They only felt moderately confident of their abilities in these areas. Interestingly, while the number of students was low, the Baltic and South Eastern European students with limited test language proficiency expressed the most confidence and use of computers for conducting academic tasks. Perhaps this group of students is using technology to counter their language deficit?

Table 7.11a **ICT and SEN students by sample**

Items & Indices	PISA				OECD					EU					Baltic & SE Countries			
	A	B	C	D	A	B	C	D	E	A	B	C	D	E	A	B	C	D
% Yes																		
Ever use computer	99	99	99	99	99	98	97	98	99	99	98	96	97	98	98	95	93	100
Use computer >5 years	48	56	58	48	60	50	51	39	54	51	45	43	35	54	36	49	21	27
Use at home daily	73	73	74	68	71	63	67	70	73	71	68	65	67	73	72	83	56	73
At school daily	10	9	9	6	11	16	15	14	6	7	12	13	10	6	5	7	20	0
At other places daily	6	6	6	7	6	6	12	11	5	6	6	11	13	5	9	7	19	7
Internet/ Entertainment Use % Daily																		
Browse	26	26	26	28	26	31	29	26	33	25	33	27	23	33	22	36	31	27
Games	26	27	28	28	27	31	38	29	38	30	35	39	32	38	36	38	42	40
Collaborate with group	20	17	17	22	17	13	18	15	27	18	16	19	14	27	14	14	23	33
Download software	21	20	23	22	21	26	25	22	30	23	27	26	20	30	30	26	31	40
Download music	36	36	36	30	37	38	38	37	38	38	37	38	35	38	9	10	19	20
Communication	50	54	52	35	50	43	46	48	43	48	40	42	45	43	30	29	32	27

Table 7.11a **ICT and SEN students by sample** (continued)

Items & Indices	PISA				OECD					EU					Baltic & SE Countries			
Programme/Software Use (% Daily)																		
Write documents	14	13	16	13	15	22	17	20	20	14	20	17	19	20	18	17	26	27
Spreadsheets	8	6	5	7	5	11	10	10	11	6	11	10	10	11	8	12	19	27
Graphics	11	11	12	12	11	20	17	15	20	12	21	18	16	20	43	41	36	40
Educational Software	8	5	4	6	4	10	9	11	7	5	10	11	10	7	11	17	22	27
Computer Programmes	11	8	8	11	8	15	15	13	11	10	17	17	14	11	47	27	32	60
Self-confidence-Internet tasks(% Well by myself)																		
Chat on-line	76	84	84	75	83	70	74	77	75	81	71	71	75	75	80	74	56	93
Search for information	86	91	92	87	91	81	80	81	82	90	80	78	78	82	42	54	33	64
Download files	76	76	79	72	77	67	63	68	71	75	63	60	67	71	54	51	41	53
Attach Files	65	71	75	63	72	60	59	64	63	67	57	54	58	63	28	27	19	33
Download music	73	76	78	65	77	63	68	76	69	74	61	66	74	69	79	76	55	73
Send emails	75	85	86	71	84	72	74	75	71	81	70	71	70	71	82	73	53	67
Self-confidence high level tasks (% Well by myself)																		
Control Viruses	40	45	46	47	44	36	43	37	58	43	38	41	35	58	85	88	66	73
Edit photos	58	60	60	51	59	53	49	54	57	58	52	48	54	58	72	68	41	80
Create databases	28	25	26	33	26	30	25	26	38	27	28	23	26	38	62	56	32	53
Copy data	76	76	79	74	77	63	63	70	75	78	64	61	71	75	76	71	47	87
Move Files	82	83	87	83	84	72	68	71	81	84	71	65	72	81	58	59	43	33
Use Word Processing	79	82	84	82	83	73	63	68	76	81	72	60	67	76	51	56	31	60
Use spreadsheets	54	49	48	66	50	41	38	38	64	52	41	38	36	64	74	73	56	60
Create presentations	61	63	64	58	62	56	47	49	58	58	53	42	46	58	38	49	38	60
Construct website	26	30	30	30	31	35	37	37	34	26	30	32	35	34	75	71	55	87
Create multimedia presentation	46	45	45	44	45	43	46	47	49	44	42	45	46	49	22	24	29	47

Codes: A: No Disability; B: Functional Disability; C: Intellectual Disability; D: Limited test language proficiency; E: Other, as designated by the National Programme Manager

Discussion

This descriptive study examined the participation and performance of Baltic and South Eastern European students with special educational needs in PISA 2006. Countries that were included in the study were: Bulgaria, Croatia, Estonia, Latvia, Lithuania, Montenegro, Romania, Serbia and Slovenia. The study design and methodology replicate previous studies that have been implemented using PISA 2003 and PISA 2006 samples for various country clusters of SEN students (*e.g.* OECD countries, EU countries, all PISA participant countries) (OECD 2007; LeRoy et al, 2008). This study described the demographic characteristics of the Baltic and South Eastern European SEN students, their beliefs and behaviours toward learning, their access and competence in information and communication technology, and their PISA performance. While the primary focus of PISA 2006 was on science competencies, mathematics and reading abilities were also examined. The performance of students with special educational needs was examined in all three academic areas, as well as in relation to typical students, socioeconomic status, and SEN samples from PISA, the OECD, and the European Union.

Overall, the percentage of PISA students within this sample who were identified as having some type of special educational need was extremely low, representing 0.65% of the PISA population in the targeted countries. Three of the nine countries (*i.e.* Bulgaria, Montenegro, and Romania) did not include SEN students in their samples. Only Lithuania's participation rate was on a par with the higher rates from other PISA countries. The whole question of participation of SEN students in PISA and how that links to exclusion rates needs further work.

As compared to their peers in other parts of the world, the SEN students from the Baltic region and the South Eastern European region all attended public schools and had larger class sizes. While vocational training opportunities were limited across the world, students in these regions had practically no such opportunities. In terms of academic performance, students in these regions performed lower than their peers, with the exception of students with limited test language proficiency, who scored higher than their peers across the world. They also reported the highest use of computers and information technology. Students in the two regions also believed that academic performance was less important than their peers in other parts of the world. Finally, with regard to information technology and computers, students in the Baltic region and in the South Eastern European region have not been using computers as long as in other regions. They use them less in school. However, they use them in the same way as other students across the world and they express more confidence in their ability to use them for high level skills.

Summary

In 2003 only two countries from the Baltic and South Eastern European regions participated in PISA (*i.e.* Latvia and Serbia-Montenegro). In 2006 nine countries from the two regions participated in PISA, with six of those nine countries including students with special educational needs in their samples. It is anticipated that an additional three countries will join PISA 2009 (*i.e.* Albania, FYROM, and Moldova). Findings from the Baltic and South Eastern European countries continue to strengthen the PISA programme. In particular, the inclusion of students with special educational needs from these regions positively contributes to this international knowledge. Data related to their demographic characteristics, school experiences, attitudes, and performance independently and within the context of other PISA regions and country reports provide an important context for other studies on special education issues. This exploratory study has provided a model upon which future research can build, as well as a baseline for comparative purposes. While the sample size for students with special educational needs was small, there are several areas in which these students' experiences differed positively from their international counterparts, such as in instructional formats and use of information and communication technology. Future studies should build on these initial findings to explore further the impact of these contextual differences on performance and school outcomes.

List of countries by sample

Baltic and South Eastern European Countries

Bulgaria, Croatia, Estonia, Latvia, Lithuania, Republic of Montenegro, Romania, Republic of Serbia, and Slovenia

OECD Countries

Australia, Austria, Belgium, Canada, Czech Republic, Denmark, Finland, France, Germany, Greece, Hungary, Iceland, Ireland, Italy, Japan, Korea, Luxembourg, Mexico, Netherlands, New Zealand, Norway, Poland, Portugal, Slovakia, Spain, Sweden, Switzerland, Turkey, United Kingdom, and the United States

European Union Countries

Austria, Belgium, Bulgaria, Czech Republic, Denmark, Estonia, Finland, France, Germany, Greece, Hungary, Ireland, Italy, Latvia, Lithuania, Luxembourg, Netherlands, Poland, Portugal, Romania, Slovakia, Slovenia, Spain, Sweden, and the United Kingdom

References

LeRoy, B., Samuel, P., Bahr, P.R., Evans, P., Deluca, M. (September 2008), PISA 2006 and the participation of students with special educational needs. Unpublished manuscript. Detroit, MI: Wayne State University.

NCEO (October 2003), Putting it all together: Including students with disabilities in assessment and accountability systems. Minneapolis, MN: National Center on Educational Outcomes, University of Minnesota.

OECD (2007), Students with disabilities, difficulties, and disadvantages – Statistics and indicators for curriculum access and equity, Paris.

OECD (2007), The participation of students with disabilities, difficulties and disadvantages in standardized assessments: The case of PISA 2003. In OECD. Students with disabilities, difficulties, and disadvantages – Statistics and indicators for curriculum access and equity (pp. 177-200), Paris.

OECD (2004a), The OECD Programme for international student assessment (PISA), Paris.

OECD (2007), PISA 2006 Science competencies for tomorrow's world, Volume 1: Analysis (pp. 28; 34-35; 43; 332; 342), Paris.

Chapter 8. Summary, Conclusions and Recommendations

This chapter provides recommendations based on the need for reforms in the education systems indicated by the data analysed in this book. Providing the correct legal framework for developing inclusive education and the necessary resources and support for students who have special education needs are important elements in developing equitable education systems where all students can benefit as fully as possible from the opportunities education brings. Gathering data is an essential component of developing effective policies and efficient strategies to achieve the goal of inclusive education and to know whether it is being achieved.

Providing the correct legal framework for developing inclusive education and the necessary resources and support for SEN students are important elements in developing equitable education systems where all students can benefit as fully as possible from the opportunities education brings. Gathering data is an essential component of developing effective policies and efficient strategies to achieve this goal and to know whether it is being achieved.

As a contribution to this effort, this book has reported work from the three different sources described below from the following economies: Bosnia and Herzegovina, Bulgaria, Croatia, Estonia, Kosovo, Latvia, Lithuania, FYRoM, Malta, Moldova, Romania, Serbia and Slovenia. First, chapters one to five provide qualitative and quantitative data based on the completion of the electronic questionnaire used by OECD to gather data in the SENDDD project, supported by DGEAC/CRELL. Second, Chapter 6 provides a more detailed account of the process through which these data are developed and gathered. This information comes from the OECD project in South Eastern Europe supplemented by work in the Baltic States and Malta supported by DGEAC/CRELL. Third, Chapter 7 gives an account of data gathered on SEN students in SEE countries and Baltic States involved in PISA 2006.

As reported in Chapters 1 to 5, the economies involved were, for the most part, readily able to provide information for the Electronic Questionnaire, both qualitatively on legal frameworks and conditions relating to special needs issues and inclusive education and quantitatively on their national categories of SEN. The legal frameworks are generally in place to support inclusive education although not all countries have signed the UN Convention on the Rights of Persons with Disabilities. What is lacking is implementation on the ground where attitudes need to be addressed and changed and skills need to be developed to allow more students to stay in school and access the curriculum. What is also lacking is a system change that would allow schools to become learning organisations through a process of adaptation to a more diverse set of student needs, including students with severe disabilities.

These economies were also able to distribute their national categories into the OECD cross-national categories of A (disabilities), B (learning and behavioural difficulties) and C (disadvantages) to facilitate international comparisons. However, as for many OECD member countries, there was a substantial amount of missing data and this clearly limits the work and the conclusions that may be drawn. Providing full data sets is an important goal to be attained in the future.

The economies were also able to provide data on the place of education, special schools, special classes and regular classes for their national categories and for the cross-national comparisons. They show substantial variation both in the proportions of students identified as well as in the place of education. For Category A the proportions identified are close to the OECD averages. However, for Category B there are substantial differences with fewer students being supported especially in upper secondary education. This is an unsatisfactory outcome and the reasons need to be identified and rectified. More investment may well be necessary at least in the short to medium terms to support these students more effectively and to provide teachers and schools with the necessary skills to help to keep them in school. More access to vocational training, which is substantially less for these countries and economies than for other EU and OECD shown by the PISA results (see Chapter 7), may well form part of the solution.

As in OECD member countries, with the exception of Lithuania, many more boys than girls are provided with additional resources to help them access the curriculum. It is unclear why. If boys genuinely need more help because education systems provide them with inherently more challenges then providing them with more resources is equitable. On the other hand, if the provision made available, *e.g.* special schools/classes, merely serves to lead to a greater likelihood of social exclusion then it is not equitable. The conclusion would be that these resources should be put into renewing regular education to prevent the systematic exclusion of many students from it as they get older as the data presented in Chapter 5 reveals.

Chapter 6 looked much more closely at the processes leading to data collection and identifies key areas for action arising from the country situation analysis. They were discussed in terms the conceptual, technical and legal issues that should be considered when developing new forms of national datasets that can be convertible for use for making international comparisons such as via the OECD tripartite taxonomy. Recommendations were made in Chapter 6 to improve data collection and quality so that important questions about participation in education for different groups of children may be answered.

The country reports reviewed as part of this process indicate many variations in the ways in which children are classified and in how data are collected. They also provide evidence of significant change and development in many of the economies concerned. The variations in responses from each of these economies to the guiding questions are sometimes difficult to interpret. In some cases the data needed to answer the questions were not available; in other cases it was not clear whether the data were not available or not provided. It is also possible that some of the questions were interpreted differently in the economies concerned. Thus the findings presented in Chapter 6 should be interpreted as partial, subject to further information gathering activities and confirmation by the participating economies.

Changes in policy and practice in many countries regarding the identification and assessment of students with SEN will result in changes to the type of data that are available to be collected. It will also expand the range of professionals who might be involved in the process. Clearly there is the need for professional development in relation to the classification process as well as support to develop systems for the handling and sharing of the data.

While there is no single method for improving data flow and for monitoring systems that applies to all of these economies, the national reports indicated high levels of awareness and urgency to improve data collection systems. In some of them, the lack of electronic databases and trained staff are a clear problem. Communication between different bodies and ministries also undermines data flow and monitoring.

Chapter 7 provides a summary of PISA 2006 data as they apply to SEN students in the economies that took part in PISA 2006 namely: Croatia, Estonia, Latvia, Lithuania, Serbia and Slovenia. In general not enough SEN students are included in PISA from not enough economies and the conclusions that can be drawn are therefore extremely limited.

In comparison to their peers in other parts of the world, the SEN students from the Baltic and the SEE regions all attended public schools and had larger class sizes. While vocational training opportunities were limited across the world, students in these regions had practically no such opportunities. In terms of academic performance, these students performed less well than their peers, with the exception of students with limited test language proficiency, who scored higher than their peers across the world. They also reported the highest use of computers and information technology. Students in the two regions also believed that academic performance was less important than their peers in other parts of the world. Finally, with regard to information technology and computers, students in these two regions have not been using computers as long as in other regions. They use them less in school. However, they use them in the same way as other students across the world and they express more confidence in their ability to use them for high level skills.

Recommendations

All of the data presented in this report indicate the need for reforms in the education systems in these economies in order for SEN students to improve outcomes and to create more equitable systems. The main themes are:

- Signing and ratifying the UN Convention on the Rights of Persons with Disabilities thus ensuring that all children are fully included in education.

- Increasing the quality of education and the supply of upper secondary and vocational training for SEN students.

- Developing a new understanding of SEN which is more in line with the social approach which permeates new thinking in this area, and creating databases which reflect this reformulation.

- Capacity development for gathering data on *ALL* children including those who are out of school. And improving the quality of the databases for students with disabilities, learning difficulties and disadvantages.

- Improving the compatibility of data between Ministries and tackling confidentiality issues.

- Understanding gender issues, that is why more boys than girls are identified.

- Involving more of these economies and more SEN students in future rounds of PISA.

Also:

- Developing inclusive education in the sense defined in OECD (1999) especially:

  - Increasing funding and redistributing it from special to regular education.

  - Developing more homogeneous provision within these economies.

  - Making schools, the curriculum and the national examination systems more accessible.

  - Finding the optimal class size to allow all of this to happen.

  - Efforts to prevent school abandonment and drop-out particularly focusing on diverse populations in school.

  - Promoting teaching methods to enable individualised teaching.

  - Promote teacher training for diversity.

  - Involving parents more fully.

More generally, providing opportunities for schools to become learning organisations would allow them to find creative solutions to challenges related to the full diversity of students abilities. Whether schools are allowed to act in this way is a major policy issue which may require reforms that relinquish some centralised control over the curriculum and school organisation.

Annex 1. EU and Accession Economies Data Returns

Qualitative and quantitative information were gathered on the following EU Member and Accession economies for the period 1999-2005:

Table A1 **EU and accession economies - data submissions**

	1999	2001	2003	2005
Austria			X	
Belgique (Fr.)		X	X	
Belgium (Fl.)	X	X	X	X
Bulgaria				X
Croatia				X
Czech Republic	X	X	X	X
Denmark	X			
Estonia				X
Finland	X	X	X	X
France	X	X		
Germany	X	X	X	X
Greece	X	X	X	
Hungary	X	X	X	X
Ireland	X			
Italy	X	X		
Latvia				X
Lithuania				X
Luxembourg		X		X
Malta				X
Netherlands	X	X	X	X
Poland	X	X		
Romania				X
Slovak Republic		X	X	X
Slovenia				X
Spain	X	X	X	X
Sweden	X	X		
United Kingdom	X	X	X	X

Annex 2. Allocation of Categories of Students with Disabilities, Learning Difficulties and Disadvantages (included in the resources definition) to Cross-National-Categories A, B and C

Bosnia Herzegovina

Cross-National Category A

1. Mild mental retardation
Children and youth with mild mental retardation are those who with expert assistance of special educator can be educated and trained for work in general and special conditions, and whose IQs is from 50 to 70.

2. Moderate mental retardation
Children and youth with moderate mental retardation are those who have difficulties in adaptive behaviour and who can be trained to do some of the simple jobs within the work process. Those children can, with the expert support, be included in local community and have IQs from 35 to 49.

3. Severe mental retardation
Children and youth with severe mental retardation are those who, with the expert support, can be trained to perform the basic hygiene skills, basic independency as well as basic socialisation. IQs from 20 to 34.

4. Profound mental retardation
Children and youth with profound mental retardation are those who need permanent care and protection in family or in special institutions. IQ is 19 or less.

5. Autism
Autism is a biological impairment of the brain that affects communication and social skills. It embeds wide spectrum of difficulties that can be graded from mild to profound.

6. Motor difficulties and chronic diseases
Children with motor difficulties are children with impairments and deformations as well as with functional or motor disabilities. These children, therefore, need protection and training for life and work in special conditions. Difficulties are present because of impairments in locomotive apparatus, central and peripheral neural system, as well as impairments resulted from chronic diseases of other systems.

7. Blindness and low vision
Blindness is condition when better eye with the maximal possible correction has visual sharpness 0.05 and less or central vision on the better eye with maximal possible correction 0.25 with narrowed field of vision from 20 degrees or less. Children with low vision are those who on a better eye with correction have visual sharpness 0.4 (40%) and less, as well as children who on a better eye with correction have visual sharpness more then 0.4 (40%) but who might experience worsening of the vision status.

8. Deafness and hearing impairments

Deaf children and youth are those who have hearing loss of 80 decibel and more and who without hearing aids cannot percept oral speech. Hard of hearing are children who have hearing loss between 25 and 80 decibel, and who cannot completely or partially percept oral speech.

9. Combined difficulties

Children and youth with combined difficulties are those who have more than one difficulty such as mental retardation, hearing impairments, visual impairments, speech and language difficulties etc.

10. Down's syndrome

11. Speech and language difficulties

Children with speech and language difficulties are those whose speech communication is impaired that much that it negatively affects psycho-physical development or rehabilitation procedure aimed at treating the difficulty and insurance of normal development, because of irreparable organic and functional changes in central and peripheral neural-muscular system.

Cross-National Category B

12. Learning difficulties

Learning difficulties are caused by organic factors or psychosis of diverse etiologies, according to medical, psychological, defectological and social expertise.

13. Attention Deficit Hyperactivity Disorder (ADHD) (Not within resources definition) Attention deficit which can be accompanied by hyperactivity is developmental impairment of self-control. ADHD imply child's behaviour which excels with by fluctuation, rapid changes of interests, and changes of activities in very short time period.

Cross-National Category C

14. Difficulties caused by socio-economic, cultural deprivation and/or caused by linguistic factors (Not within resources definition) Learning difficulties caused by socio-economic, cultural deprivation and/or caused by linguistic factors embed the children who have learning difficulties caused by: poverty, different cultural background and/or language barriers in comparison with other children (national minorities)

Bulgaria

Cross-National Category A

1. Students with mental retardation

Children and students with slow or incomplete development of intellectual abilities, connected with disorders of all basic abilities needed for common intelligence, *e.g.* cognitive, speech, language, motor and social. This may be combined with other physical or psychological disorders.

2. Students with hearing impairments

Children and students with hearing loss over 30 dB, which hampers discrimination of sounds, processing of linguistic information and development of speech, language and communication abilities. This causes different social consequences for the individual - in learning, socialisation, communication, re-adaptation, re-integration, etc.

3. Students with visual impairments

Children and students with disabilities in visual activities, which they face during completion of visual tasks in certain conditions from the point of view of other people. This causes different social consequences for the child – in learning, socialisation, communication with other people, need of re-adaptation, re-integration, etc.

4. Students with speech-language disorders

Children and students with serious speech, language and communication disorders, such as stuttering, developmental dyslexia, specific language disorders, articulation disorders, voice disorders and others, *e.g.* disorders of all processes, connected with understanding and production of spoken and written language and verbal and non-verbal communication, which makes for difficulties in learning and education.

5. Students with physical impairments

Children and students with different disorders of the loco-motor system, such as cerebral palsy, etc. They reflect on the physics of body with different consequences. They may vary from mild without serious consequences, to severe with physical impairments which need re-adaptation, re-socialisation, re-integration, etc.

6. Students with multiple disorders

Children and students with multiple disorders, for example blind-deaf, blind with physical impairments and others. The disorders may be severe and cause different social consequences for the child - in learning, socialisation, and communication with other people, need of re-adaptation and re-integration, etc.

7. Students with autism

Children and students with a type of generalised development disorder defined by the presence of abnormal and/or impaired development which can be seen in the abnormal type of functioning of the following three areas: social relations, communication, and behaviour, which are limited and stereotypical.

Cross-National Category B

8. Students with learning difficulties

Children and students with difficulties in psychic processes which causes difficulties with understanding and use of spoken and written language. They have difficulties with thinking, speech, reading, writing, and mathematical operations. The problem may causes critical disparity between the child's potential and his progress.

9. Students with psychological disorders

Children and students with hyperkinetic disorders, which are characterised by an early beginning; a combination of hyperactive behaviour with emphasized inadvertence and a lack of firm participation in solving tasks; generalization of those characteristics in different situations in time.

Children and students with behaviour disorders, which are characterised by a repetitive and stable model of unsocial, aggressive, or provocative behaviour .

Children and students with emotional and behaviour disorders, which are characterised by a combination of aggressive, unsocial, and provocative behaviour with evident symptoms of depression, anxiety, and other emotional disorders.

Cross-National Category C

10. Students with other difficulties due to social reasons
Children and students with educational skill disorders, emotional and behaviour problems due to bilingualism, immigrant families, problematic family environment, institutionalization, etc.

Croatia

Cross-National Category A

1. Visual impairment
Visual impairment includes blindness and amblyopia. A blindness is considered when a visual acuity of 0.10 (10%) is obtained by using corrective glass and also when using corrective glass up to 0.25 (25%) is necessary for central sight at better eye, but the eye field is reduced for 20 degree and less. The education in Braille alphabet is necessary when the visual remain at better eye is 0.05 (5%) with corrective glass or regardless visual acuity and reading disability of letters and characters Jeager size 8 in a short distance. The amblyopia means the visual acuity at better eye with corrective glass of 0.4 (40%) and less.

2. Hearing impairment
Hearing impairment includes deafness and hearing loss. The deafness is considered as a loss of 81 decibels and more and a person without hearing apparatus cannot completely recognize voices. The hearing loss is considered a hearing impairment from 25 to 80 decibels at ear with better hearing and when the verbal speaking is partially or almost completely developed

4. Physical disability
For physical disabilities as impairment, deformations, functional or motoric difficulties there is need to provide protection and enabling appropriate life and work conditions. The causes of this condition are: a) impairments of loco-motor system, b) impairments of central nervous system, c) impairments of peripheral nervous system, and d) impairments as a result of chronic diseases of other systems.

5. Mental retardation
Mental retardation is a state with difficulties regarding inclusion to social life, in a relation with interrupted or uncompleted intellectual development defined by means of medical, psychological, defectological and social expertise. Intellectual level examined by instruments is approximate to Wechsler type of 0 to 69 if an outstanding emotional lability is not defined. The mental retardation levels are: a) minor mental retardation, IQ within 50 to 69, b) mild mental retardation, IQ within 35 to 49, c) rather severe mental retardation, IQ within 20 to 34, d) severe mental retardation demanding continuous care and protection. Depending on ability grade, the most elemental habits could be reached by applying an appropriate rehabilitation, IQ within 0 to 20.

6. Organic conditioned behaviour dysfunctions
Behavioural disorders by organic factors or progressive psychopathological condition
Behaviour dysfunctions conditioned by an organic factor or by progressive psychopathological condition based on medical, psychological, pedagogic and social expertise should be enabled for life and work within appropriate conditions and for implementing appropriate socio-protective forms.

7. Autism
Autism is a condition of emotional, intelligence, psycho-motorical, verbal and social communication disability. The basic characteristic of autism is a self-retirement, voice-speaking communication dysfunction and aimless activity and perseveration.

8. Other visual impairment
All other visual impairment which is not blindness and amblyopia.

11. Health problems
Health dysfunctions difficulties category includes students suffering epilepsy, heart and blood vessel disease, gastrointestinal disease, uric disease, respiratory disease, endocrine disease, psychiatric disease, elective mutism and chronic diseases that are reason of longer medical treatment.

Cross-National Category B

3. Dysfunctions of speaking and voice communication (speech and language disabilities)
Dysfunctions of speaking and voice communication (voice, speaking, language, reading, writing) are those where exist regarding speaking communication or where the speaking communication does not exist because of non-renewable organic and functional changes in central and peripheral neuromuscular system, so it is necessary to provide conditions for training and protection..

9. Specific learning difficulties/Other dysfunctions of speaking and voice communication
Other dysfunctions of speaking and voice communication like alkalis, stammer etc. Specific learning difficulties regarding: reading (dyslexia, alexsia), writing (disgraphia, agraphia) and calculating (discalculia, acalculia)

10. Reduced cognitive function/Remedial Education
Reduced cognitive function category includes students having lower learning score, learning difficulties or student that teachers additionally work with attending remedial teaching.

12. Behaviour problems
It includes students who violate younger and weaker students (knowledge of professional development school department), blackmail and extort, physically or verbal aggressive, frequently lie, steal, destroy things, interfere with lesson, students who do not respect adults, who are self-aggressive, who have harmful friendships and go out after 11 p.m. (forbidden for children under age of 16), or students whose behaviour or unfair absence was the reason for getting reproof.

13. Hyperactivity and attention deficit (not in the resources definition)
It includes students whose concentration is somewhat difficult or they are not focused on their tasks.

14. Addictions (not in the resources definition)
The category of addictions includes students who consume alcohol, drugs and tobacco.

Cross-National Category C

15. Other difficulties/disadvantages (not in the resources definition)
Other disadvantages include social deprivation and emotional difficulties.

16. Institutional accommodations (not in the resources definition)
It includes students who live in students' house during their education, students who live in children's centres for social reason, students who live in trustee family and students who live in correctional institution.

17. Family problems
This category includes students from families that are characterised by dysfunctional relations which significantly influence the living conditions of students. (not in the resources definition)

18. Language dysfunctions (Second language)

This category includes bilingual students, national minority students, students with insufficient knowledge or Croatian language, Romany students.

Estonia

Cross-National Category A

1. Students with intellectual disability

Students with intellectual disability are students whose learning ability is limited and who need simplified curriculum or curriculum for students with moderate and severe intellectual disability.

4. Students with mental health problems

Students with mental health problems are students who have cognitive or emotional or psychiatric disorders or autistic spectrum disorders and need special methodology and additional support staff in a learning process.

5. Students with multiple disabilities

Students with multiple disabilities are students who have severe hearing and visual impairment, also students with moderate visual, hearing, speech and physical impairment, who have limited learning ability due to moderate, severe or profound intellectual disability.

6. Students with hearing impairment

Students with hearing impairment are students who due to their hearing loss have inability to hear or distinguish among different sounds and therefore will have problems in speech and language development to an extent that needs specialist support, special methodology, extended study-time or individual approach.

7. Students with visual impairment

Students who have a loss of vision that constitutes a significant limitation of visual capability or visual functions to an extent that they need special teaching methodology, adapted study materials, extended study-time or an individualised approach in teaching.

8. Students with speech impairment

Students who have an impaired ability to produce speech sounds or who have problems with voice quality to an extent that needs special methodology, extended study-time or an individualised approach.

9. Students with physical disabilities

Students with limitations due to their skeleto-muscular system necessitating physical aids, special methodologies, an individualised approach or an especially adapted physical environment.

11. Students with chronic and progressive diseases

Students with chronic and progressive diseases are students who suffer from chronic and progressive diseases or who due to long term illness have not been able to attend regular school, need medical monitoring or special support to fulfil curriculum requirements.

Cross-National Category B

2. Students with learning difficulties
Students who in spite of support and consultations from subject and class teachers are not able to fulfill curriculum requirements.

3. Students with specific learning difficulties
Students who experience deficits in any area of information processing that can manifest in a variety of specific learning difficulties - deficits in reading, difficulties with written expression or difficulties in learning math concepts.

10. Students with behavioural difficulties
Students who have serious social, emotional or behavioural problems and need special conditions, special methodology and additional support staff to achieve study results according to their abilities.

12. Students with temporary learning difficulties
Students whose difficulties can be overcome with the help of support services (corrective teaching, individual learning plan, speech therapy, adapted study materials). Part-time remedial teaching.

15. Gifted students (not applicable)
Students who have very good learning or academic results and who need adapted study materials and individual learning in order to develop their general or specific intellectual and academic abilities.

Cross-National Category C

13. Students with accommodation difficulties
Students who due to health problems or change of domicile need adapted study methods, study materials or specialist support in order to restore study results according to their abilities.

14. Immigrant students
Persons who have lived in Estonia less than 3 years and whose level of knowledge of the state language hinders acquisition of study material according to his/her abilities and who therefore needs additional support with adapted study materials, methodology and additional language studies.

Kosovo (UNMIK – PISG)

Cross-National Category A

1. Intellectual impairment
Persons with intellectual impairments are those who have the intellectual level evidently under the average level beside their group ages, have difficulties in learning and social adaptation in different levels. Retard definition of mental-lags/ intellectual impairment. Mental light retardation level IQ from 70to 55/50. Mental retardation middle-moderated level IQ from 55/50 to 40/35. Mental hard retardation level IQ from 40/35 to 25/20. Mental retardation very hard level of IQ under 25/20.

Mental retardation refers to substantial intellectual delay that requires environmental or personal supports to live independently. Mental retardation is manifested by below-average intellectual functioning in two or more life areas (work, education, daily living, etc.) and is present before the age of 18.

Intellectual impairment refers to substantial limitations in present functioning. It is characterised by:

- significantly sub-average intellectual functioning, existing concurrently with
- related limitations in two or more of the following applicable adaptive skill areas:
  - o communication
  - o self-care
  - o home living
  - o social skills
  - o community use
  - o self-direction
  - o health and safety
  - o functional academics
  - o leisure
  - o work
  - o which manifest before age 18.

It is important to remember that there is as much diversity of characteristics, abilities and needs among people with intellectual impairment as there is within the general population.

2. Hearing impairment

Hearing impairment implies continuous reduction in voice hearing that obstruct the verbal communication. Hearing impaired persons are classified into half deaf and deaf persons. 1. In the half deaf category are those persons whose the verge of best ear 25-80dB have developed fully speaking or partly. According to the level of impairment we have classified in this way a) hearing light impaired persons 20-40 dB b) hearing mid impaired persons 40-60 dB c) persons with hard hearing impairments 60-80dB. d) Deaf persons are considered hearing impairment that is up to 80 dB.

Deaf refers to a profound degree of hearing loss that prevents understanding speech through the ear. Hearing impaired or hearing loss are generic terms used by some individuals to indicate any degree of hearing loss-from mild to profound. These terms include people who are hard of hearing and deaf. However, some individuals completely disfavor the term hearing impaired. Others prefer to use deaf or hard of hearing. Hard of hearing refers to a mild to moderate hearing loss that may or may not be corrected with amplification.

3. Visual impairment

1. Partly visual indicate few kinds of visual problems by which result in the need for special education.

2. "Weak visual impairment refers to the hard visual impairment, not necessary limited looking in a distance. Weak visual impairment is used for all visual persons who are not able to read the newspaper in a normal distance of sight even with glasses or eyeglasses. When they read they use the visual combination and other senses, although it is appropriate with brighten or the size of letters and sometimes use the Braille.

3. According to the "Law" 'blind' indicate that person has a lower visual than 6/60 in the best eye or a very limited visual field (20 grades in the wider point).

4. Students completely blind learn through Braille or other media- non visual. Normal visual 6/60, weak visual impairment <6/18 to > 3/60, very weak visual impairment (blind) <3/60 visual field <20 grade blind according to law.

Blind describes a condition in which a person has loss of vision for ordinary life purposes. Visually impaired is the generic term used by some individuals to refer to all degrees of vision loss.

4. Physical impairment
Physical impairment include congenital impairment (born) or gained of muscles, nerves, bones or skin which reduce remove or difficulties in carrying out daily activities such as: movement, personal care, clothes, food, cleaning etc.

Physical impairment as a musculoskeletal (involving the joints, limbs and associated muscles) and/or neurological (involving the central nervous system, *i.e.* brain, spinal cord or peripheral nerves) condition which affects the ability to move or to coordinate the control movement.

5. Multiple impairments
A multiple impaired person has a combination of two or more impairments. Multiple impairment persons are considered as persons with hard impairment.

6. Autism
Autism is a development disorder that characterises qualitative impairment of reciprocal social qualitative interactions, nonverbal communication, verbal imagination and limited number of activities and interest. Autism is showed prior to age 3.

Autism is a mental disorder originating in infancy that is characterised by absorption in self-centred subjective mental activity, especially when accompanied by marked withdrawal from reality, inability to interact socially, repetitive behaviour, and language dysfunction.

Cross-National Category B

7. Emotional disorders
This is a condition exhibiting one or more of the following characteristics over a long period of time and to marked degree that adversely affects a child's educational performance:

(A) An inability to learn that cannot be explained by intellectual, sensory, or health factors.
(B) An inability to build or maintain satisfactory interpersonal relationships with peers and teachers.
(C) Inappropriate types of behaviour or feelings under normal circumstances.
(D) A general pervasive mood of unhappiness or depression.
(E) A tendency to develop physical symptoms or fears associated with personal or school problems.

Latvia

Cross-National Category A

1. Disabilities of mental development (mental retardation)
Mild mental retardation IQs 50-69; moderate - IQs 35-49; severe - IQs 24-34; profound - IQ 23 and less; and other conditions with corresponding IQs.

3. Visual impairments
(21015111/21)Acuity of vision with correction in the best eye is in the limits of 0-0.2; taking into consideration conditions of other functions of vision (visual angle 20 grades acuity of vision in proximity and necessity to use specially designed vision correction materials); other forms of pathological processes and their dynamics.

4. Hearing impairments
(21015211/21)Sensory neurological and conductive hearing impairments (levels 2-5), deaf and hard of hearing; children with cochlear implants and mild hearing disabilities.

5. Physical disabilities
(21015311/21)Congenial or acquired physical deformities and affections of support and movement system of the body; neurological patients with physical disabilities

7. Mental health disorders
(21015711/21)Mental disabilities, behavioural and emotional problems due to brain ailment or damage; mental illnesses, temper disorders; disorders connected to stress; pervasive developmental disabilities; severe cases of epilepsy.

8. Chronic health problems (somatic illnesses)
(21015411/21) Illnesses of digestive organs, diabetes (type 1), students with tuberculosis (TB) (all kinds of the disease); children who have been in contact with patient of active TB; students with non-specific lung diseases - asthma, chronic bronchitis, situations after lung operations, recurrent pneumonia, allergies like hay-fever.

Cross-National Category B

2. Learning disabilities
(21015611/21) Specific learning difficulties - reading disabilities, writing difficulties, difficulties in calculating skills, mild cognitive disabilities

6. Speech and language disabilities
(21015501/21) Insufficient development of speech and language system (levels 1-2), phonetic phonematic disabilities; specific reading, writing disabilities; specific speech articulation disabilities; disabilities of expressive language.

10. Pedagogical correction/ Remedial Teaching
(2101) Students who due to different reasons (health problems, truancy, insufficient learning etc.) have not acquired the education standards.

Cross-National Category C

9. Disadvantaged background
(Residential schools) (21011111/21) Pupils from disadvantaged background – poor families, abusive homes, orphans, children who have no parents' custody.

Lithuania

Cross-National Category A

1. Intellectual disorders
A mental capability deviation which generates behavioural, emotional and socialization disorders. (IQ below 70, measured by WISC-III test adapted to Lithuania).

5. Hearing disorders
A mild hearing disorder is considered to be equal to 26-40 dB of hearing loss. There are various levels of hearing loss. Hearing is assessed and evaluated by a medical doctor.

6. Visual disorders
Visual disorders – low vision is considered to be when a person's visual acuity with maximum of possible optical correction is equal or less than 0.3 or his/her visual field is equal or less than 60 degrees. There are levels of visual loss from a low vision till practical blindness. Vision is assessed by a medical doctor.

7. Movement disorders
Physical disorders. Physical conditions are assessed and evaluated by a medical doctor. These disorders might be inborn or caused by illness or physical trauma. Not always a student with such a disorder needs additional resources in educational system.

8. Somatic and neurological disorders
Chronic somatic and neurological disorders. Disorders of a heart and blood supply system, breathing, digesting, epilepsy etc.

9. Complex disorders
These are combinations of two or more disorders that belong to other groups of disorders. For example, intellectual disorder and visual impairment.

Cross-National Category B

2. Specific learning difficulties
Specific cognitive disorders (*e.g.* attention, memory, visual or auditory perception disorders) caused by a minor brain dysfunction but definitely not by intellectual disorder, social disadvantages, visual or hearing impairment. In this case a student might be highly intelligent but nevertheless experiencing problems in reading, writing or mathematics.

3. Emotional, behaviour and socialisation disorders
Attention deficit hyperactivity disorder, hypo activity (extreme slowness), behaviour disorder, various disorders of emotional health (phobias, anxiety, aggressiveness etc.

4. Speech and other communication disorders
A deviance appears in speech, language and communication of a student to compare to common or usually used speech and communication. But this disorder is not caused by intellectual, visual or hearing disorders.

Cross-National Category C

10. Other disorders
All disorders that are not covered by the former 9 groups (*e.g.* developmental disorders caused by a psychological and pedagogical neglecting of a child).
Students who belong to this group usually have a lot of special educational needs therefore additional resources are needed.

Malta

Cross-National Category A

1. Intellectual Disability
Mild to profound and includes: Auditory short-term memory, brain damage, Brain Encephalitis, Cognitive Delay/Impairment, Developmental & general delay in cognitive functioning, Down Syndrome, Fragile-X-Syndrome, Global Intellectual Impairment, Hyperkinetic Syndrome, Idiopathic Hypercalcaemia, Learning Difficulties, Mental retardation, Microcephalus, Phenylketonuria/PKU/GDD, Severe Hyper Kinetic Conduct Disorder, Significant Literacy Difficulties, Slow learner, Trisomy 21, West Syndrome.

4. Communication Difficulty
Aspergers Syndrome, Autistic Disorder, Communication Problems, Motor and Linguistic Difficulties, Pervasive Developmental Disorder, Phonological Speech Disorder, Speech/language Delay.

5. Sensory Difficulties
Charge Syndrome, Congenital Insensitivity to Pain, Duane's Syndrome, Hearing Impairment, Prosthetic Eye, and Visual Impairment.

6. Physical Disability
Achondroplasia, Albinism, Arthrogryposis, Autoimmune Entheropathy, Central Hypoventilation Syndrome, Cerebral Dysfunction, Cerebral Palsy, Complex Congenital Heart Disease, Crouzon's Syndrome, Dopa Responsive Dystonia, Dopamine Responsive Hypotonia, Dopsa N. Dystonia, Duchenne Muscular Dystrophy, Dwarfism, Dystonis, Epilepsy, Epileptic Dyslexia, Epileptic Fits, Gastric Problems, Gait Disorder, Hemiplegia, Hirscufprung Disease, HMSM, Hydrocephalus, Hypersensitive to Nuts, Hyperthyroidism, Hypochondroplasia, Hypoplastic Cerebellum, Hypoxic Ischemia Spastic, Infantile Hydrocephal, Krabbe Syndrome, L. Dopa, Leucodystrophy, Lumbosacral Myelemeningocoele, Metatrophic Dysplasia, Nasal Encephalocoele, Nephrotic Syndrome, Obstetrical Brachial Plexus Palsy, Osteogenesis Imperfecta, Optic Nerve Hypoplesia & Abnormal Spinal Curve, Optiz Syndrome, Perthe's Disease, Pierre Robin Syndrome, R. Femur Deficiency, Recurrent Iron Convulsions, Russel Silver Syndrome, Sacral Agensis, Segawa Dystonia, Spastic Diplegia, Spina Bifida, Spinal Tumor, Tufting Enteropathy, Vater Syndrome, VP Shunt with Hydrocephalus, Worster Drough Syndrome.

7. Multiple Disability
Acrocallosal Syndrome, Aicardi-Goutieres Syndrome, Alagille Syndrome Disorder, Angelman Syndrome, Cornelia de Lange Syndrome, Cri du chat, Dandy Walker Syndrome, Global Developmental Delay, Idiopathic Congenital Nystagmus, Lennox Gastaut Syndrome, Myalgic Encephaloyelitis (Chronic Fatigue Syndrome), Moebius Syndrome, Multiple Disabilities, Neurofibro-matosis, Noonam Syndrome, Prader-Willi Syndrome, Rett Syndrome, Rommer-Mueller-Sybert Syndrome, Spastic Condition becasue of Tuberous Sclerosis, Tuberous Sclerosis Complex (TSC), Tourette Syndrome, Williams Syndrome.

Cross-National Category B

2. Specific Learning Difficulty
Dyslexia, Dyspraxia

3. Emotional and Behavioural Difficulty
Aggressive Behaviour Problems, Anxiety at school, Attention Deficit Disorder, Attention Deficit Hyperactivity Disorder, Behavioural problems, Emotional and Behavioural Difficulties (EBD),

Emotional Disturbance, Hyperactive, Immature Behaviour, Not Coping, Oppositional Defiant Disorder (ODD), Psychological Problems, School Phobia, Socio-emotional & Cognitive Development, Trauma.

Moldova

NOT PROVIDED

Montenegro

Cross-National Category A

1. Children with physical disabilities
Children with permanent physical disabilities, locomotor disorders, hard muscular disorders, cerebral palsy, etc.
a) Light invalid children
b) Moderate invalid children
c) Hard invalid children
d) Severe invalid children

2. Children with intellectual disabilities
Children with delay in intellectual development (basically or secondary origin). Due to that they have difficulties in general maturity and capabilities for learning and adopting of every day skills.
a) Children with light disorders in mental development
b) Children with moderate disorders in mental development
c) Children with hard disorders in mental development
d) Children with severe disorders in mental development

3. Children with visual impairments
Children with visual impairments are blind children and children with visual disorders.
a) Weak sight children
b) Moderate sight children
c) Hard sight children
d) Blind children
e) Blind children with residual sight.

4. Children with hearing impairments
a) Children with a minor loss of hearing
b) Children with limited loss of hearing
c) Children with more severe loss of hearing
d) Children with a severe loss of hearing
e) Children with most severe loss of hearing
f) Children with a complete loss of hearing

5. Children with speech difficulties
Children with speech difficulties are children with light difficulties in verbal expressions, using of speech functions, which are not hearing consequences. Difficulties have manifestations in speech understanding, verbal expressions, etc.
a) Children with light speech problems
b) Children with moderate speech problems
c) Children with hard speech problems
d) Children with hardest speech problems

6. Children with hard chronically diseases

Areas of difficulties: cardiologic, endocrinology (diabetes mellitus etc.) gastroenterological, aerologic, rheumatologic, auto (lupus etc.), nefrological, pulmological (asthma, etc.) hematological (anemia, leukemia, malign tumors etc.) dermatovencrological, psychiatrist (psychosis, autism, etc.) neurological (epilepsy etc.).

7. Children with combined difficulties

Children with combined difficulties are those children who have a combination of two or more disabilities or disorders described in other categories. These students follow the curriculum according to their primary difficulty.

8. Children with long-term diseases

Chronically ill children are those children who have a disease which lasts longer than three months, of different origin.

Cross-National Category B

9. Children with behavioural problems

Children with dissocial behaviours which are intensive, permanent and continued. They generate unsuccessful social integration. Dissocial behaviour could be with internal or external reasons, and manifest in: aggression, self-aggression, drug and alcohol addiction, etc.

10. Children with emotional problems

Children with anxious disorders, separation problems from early childhood, phobias, fears, etc.

11. Children with learning difficulties

Children with learning difficulties which are connected with attention, cognition, memory, concentration, development of social skills, problems in reading, writing, calculating (dyslexia, dyscalculia, disgrafia etc.). Basically they are not related with sensor, physically, intellectual or emotional.

Cross-National Category C

12. Social disadvantages

Groups: Roma, institutionalised orphans, abused children, language barriers.

Romania

NOT PROVIDED

Serbia

Cross-National Category A

1. Bodily invalid children

They are divided into three subgroups:
- children with severe and permanent disorders or damage to the locomotor system, and with serious and permanent bodily deformity;
- children with severe muscular diseases and damage (cerebral palsy, muscular dystrophy, multiple sclerosis);
- children with severe forms of chronic diseases and permanently impaired health;

2. Blind students

A child is considered to be blind:

- if he/she has no sense of light,
- if his/her better eye has a remnant of vision of 0.05 with the help of a corrective lens;
- if his/her functional ability to see is so reduced that it prevents education by means of eyesight;

A child has impaired eyesight if his/her sharpness of vision in the better eye is less than 0.4 with the help of a corrective lens.

3. Deaf students

A deaf child

- is one whose hearing impairment is over 90 decibels and who cannot hear speech even with the help of a hearing aid; depending on the age at which the child became deaf and the degree of speech development, there exist four subgroups:
- a child who developed speech ability before losing his/her hearing and still speaks well at the moment of classification;
- a child who developed speech ability before hearing impairment set in, but has partially forgotten his/her speech due to a lack of practice;
- a child who became deaf before developing his/her speech and has partially developed speech owing to special practice;
- a child who became deaf before developing his/her speech and did not develop it afterwards, thus becoming deaf and mute;

4. Mentally retarded children

Children with cognitive problems. Mentally retarded children may be divided into four subgroups.

- slight/mild mental retardation (IQ does not exceed 70, can be professionally trained and enabled for work under special conditions);
- moderate mental retardation (IQ does not exceed 50, capable of being educated under special conditions; can be trained to perform simple work and to adapt to the basic requirements of the environment he/she lives in);
- serious/severe mental retardation (IQ does not exceed 35, able to develop elementary hygienic habits and to serve him/herself and to perform very simple work);
- severe/profound mental retardation (IQ below 20, very limited mental ability and activity).

5. Pupils at hospital/home treatment

Pupils are at longer hospital/home treatment

9. Autism

Children having problems in the development of social skills and communication as well as problems in cognitive development.

Cross-National Category B

6. Writing difficulties

Serious problems with writing, pupil cannot properly write letters and words, dysgrafia.

7. Reading difficulties

Pupils cannot read words, sentences, texts (dyslexia).

8. Hyperkinetic syndrome

Intensive motoric activities, inability to keep attention or stay at one place.

Cross-National Category C

10. Difficulties caused by linguistic and cultural deprivation and socio-economic factors
Roma pupils and other minorities. Children who are socially and economically deprived.

Slovenia

Cross-National Category A

1. Children with a mild mental disability
a) Children with a mild mental disability:
the child exhibits lower learning abilities. In adapted learning conditions they can achieve basic academic knowledge, which, however, does not guarantee the acquisition of the minimal knowledge standards required by the educational programmes. If appropriately educated, they can be trained to carry out less demanding vocational work and lead an independent social life.

2. Children with a moderate, severe and profound mental disability
b) Children with a moderate mental disability:
the child exhibits differently developed individual abilities. As far as academic learning is concerned, they can acquire basic reading, writing and arithmetic skills, while in other areas (movement, visual art, music) they can achieve more. They are capable of participating in simple conversation and can understand instructions. They are also able to use substitute communication and can communicate their needs and wishes. In managing their own life, they can successfully carry out simple tasks but need guidance and different levels of support throughout their life. They can be trained to carry out simple practical tasks but can only exceptionally become trained to lead a completely independent life.

c) Children with a severe mental disability:
the child can be trained to carry out the simplest of tasks. In managing their own life they frequently need the assistance of others. They understand simple messages and can respond to them. They are able to orient themselves within the narrower environment but need assistance. Children with a severe mental development disorder may exhibit difficulties in movement, other disorders and illnesses.

d) Children with profound mental disability:
the child can be trained to participate only in individual activities. They need constant care, protection, assistance and guidance. They are limited in movement; there are additional severe disorders, illnesses and diseases. The understanding and following of instructions is very limited.

3. Children with visual impairments and blind
Blind and visually impaired children are children with an impaired sight, eye or visual field.

A) Visually impaired child
A visually impaired child exhibits acuity values from 0.30 to 0.10, or acuity less than 0.10 to 0.05, or a narrowed visual field of 20 degrees or less around the fixation point regardless of acuity.
With regard to visual impairment we distinguish:

a) Moderately visually impaired children: the child has 10% – 30% sight and learns on the basis of methods for visually impaired children. The speed of work can equal the speed of seeing children. Some visually impaired children can see on the board. They need special knowledge about the use of aids.

b) Severely visually impaired children: the child has 5% – 9.9% sight and uses residual sight. They need textbooks in enlarged print. Adjustments depend on the individual characteristics of the impairment. Appropriate lighting is of utmost importance. They exhibit difficulties in handling small objects and in the observation of remote phenomena and objects. In everyday life they can be independent if sufficiently careful and in possession of specific skills. In school they learn on the basis of methods for visually impaired children but are slower.

B) Blind child

A blind child exhibits an acuity of less than 0.05 to 0.02, or a narrowed visual field around the fixation point from 5 to 10 degrees regardless of the acuity, or an acuity of less than 0.02 to the perception of light and a narrowed visual field around the fixation point up to 5 degrees regardless of acuity or acuity of 0 (amaurosis).

With regard to blindness we distinguish:

a) Blind children with some residual sight: the child has 2% – 4.9% sight and can use sight to recognise small objects at the distance of 1-2 m. Besides developing other sense organs, they must systematically develop their residual sight. They need ongoing special training for managing their everyday life, adapted learning aids and aids for blind persons. In order to be able to move around and work they need appropriate lighting, contrasts etc. In school, they learn on the basis of the combined method; mainly in Braille, with the help of different magnifiers also visually.

b) Blind children with the minimum residual sight (light projection – 1.9% sight): the child sees shadows, contours of large objects (projection), objects in the size of fingers can be recognised at the distance of up to 1 m (ca 1.9% sight). In everyday life they learn and acquire skills in the same way as completely blind persons. They need ongoing special training, adapted learning aids and aids for blind persons so as to orient themselves and also for everyday life. They write in Braille. The blind child with the minimum residual sight, identified at the upper limit defining this group, can read greatly enlarged letters. Next to developing other sense organs, they must systematically develop their residual sight.

c) Completely blind children (amaurosis): the child must use other sense organs in everyday life as well as for academic work. They are limited in their exploration of the environment and in actively participating in it. If properly treated, they can on average become equal to their seeing peers in the formation of abstract concepts and in other aspects of development. They need constant special training for coping with their everyday life, adapted teaching aids and aids for blind persons in order to orient themselves and for everyday life. They write in Braille.

4. Children with hearing impairments and deaf

Deaf and hearing impaired children exhibit impairments which include the ear, its structure and functions connected with it.

A) Hearing impaired child

A hearing impaired child exhibits on average a loss of hearing at the frequencies of 500, 1 000 and 2 000 Hertz (Hz), less than 91 decibels (dB) and has serious problems listening to speech and with speech communication. Hard-of-hearingness means the narrowing of the hearing field which partially interferes with the communication based on speech.

With regard to hard-of-hearingness we distinguish:

a) Children with a mild loss of hearing (26–40 dB): the child suffers from a profound or severe hearing loss in one ear and a mild loss or no loss in the other ear. They can also suffer from a mild hearing loss in both ears. Communication and listening to speech is affected. Other kinds of listening impairments might also be present. The child's orientation is affected.

b) Children with a moderate hearing loss (41–55 dB): the child suffers from a moderate hearing loss in both ears, complete hearing loss in one ear and a mild loss or no loss at all in the other ear, or a profound hearing loss in one ear and moderate, mild or no loss in the other ear. Communication and listening to speech might be affected, or there may be other kinds of listening disabilities. Behavioural disorders and disabilities connected with knowledge acquisition can also be present. The child is impaired in orientation and physical autonomy.

c) Children with a severe hearing loss (56–70 dB): the child suffers from a severe hearing loss in both ears or a profound hearing loss in one ear and a severe hearing loss in the other ear. Their communication is affected, as well as the understanding of speech and listening to speech. A simultaneous behavioural disorder, disabilities in knowledge acquisition and in the adaptation of one's behaviour to the circumstances can also be present. The child with a severe hearing loss is impaired in orientation, inclusion in the society and in physical autonomy.

d) Children with a profound hearing loss (71–90 dB): the child suffers from a complete hearing loss in one ear and a severe hearing loss in the other ear or from a profound hearing loss in both ears. Communication, especially the understanding of and listening to speech, is affected. Frequently there are also behavioural disorders, disabilities in adapting one's behaviour to the circumstances and in knowledge acquisition. The child is impaired in orientation, physical autonomy and in inclusion in the society.

B) Deaf child

A deaf child suffers from the most profound hearing loss, where the amplification of sound is of no avail. The average hearing loss at the frequencies of 500, 1 000 and 2 000 Hertz (Hz) amounts to 91 decibels (dB) and more.

With regard to deafness we distinguish:

a) Children with the most profound hearing loss (91 decibels or more): the child with the most profound hearing loss is not capable of hearing and understanding speech even when amplified. They cannot fully internalize speech even with a hearing aid. The impairment in communication, the understanding of and listening to speech are all present as well as other listening disabilities. Frequently there are concurrent behavioural disorders, disabilities connected with the orientation in time and space, in the adaptation of one's behaviour to the circumstances and in the acquisition of knowledge. The child is impaired in orientation, physical autonomy and inclusion in the society.

b) Children with a complete hearing loss: the child with a complete hearing loss can differentiate neither between two sound levels nor between two frequencies, and is further not capable of hearing or understanding speech even when it is amplified. They cannot internalise speech even with a hearing aid. Communication, the understanding of and listening to speech as well as other listening impairments are present. Frequently there are concurrent behavioural disorders, disabilities connected with the orientation in time and space, in the adaptation of one's behaviour to the circumstances and in the acquisition of knowledge. The child is impaired in orientation, physical autonomy and inclusion in the society.

5. Children with speech and language disorders

Children with speech and language disorders exhibit disorders in learning and comprehension as well as in speech production, which are not the consequences of a hearing loss. The disorders can be observed in the comprehension of speech and in speech and language production, and they range from mild retardation to underdevelopment. Specific disorders in the area of comprehension, structuring, processing and articulation can also be observed in the disharmony between their verbal and non-verbal abilities. Secondary disorders in speech and language communication can be seen in the area of reading, writing and learning in general. The functional reading and writing knowledge can be affected, spanning from mild retardation to functional illiteracy.

With regard to speech and language disorders we distinguish:
a) Children with mild speech and language disorders: the child's speech and language communication deviates from the average of the children of the same chronological age in one of the areas: articulation, structure or semantics. They are capable of using a demanding multi-modal substitute and supplementary communication.

b) Children with moderate speech and language disorders: the disorders in the area of speech and language communication prevent the child from successfully communicating with the environment. The delay in speech and language development can be observed in all areas: articulation, morphology, semantics and syntax. They are able to use the multi-modal substitute and supplementary communication. Written communication is limited.

c) Children with severe speech and language disorders: child's communication is very limited, it depends on the persons from the narrower environment. They need constant guidance and various levels of assistance. They are capable of using simple substitute and supplementary communication, which enables them to communicate with persons from the narrower environment.

d) Children with profound speech and language disorders: the child responds only to situations and communicates mostly with body language. The use of substitute and supplementary communication is restricted to repeated situations and for satisfying one's most basis needs. Concrete objects are used for communication.

6. Children with physical disabilities
Children who are impaired in their movements have either innate or acquired impairments, a damaged movement system, or have suffered damages in the central or peripheral nervous system. The impairment can be observed in the form of functional and movement disorders.

With regard to movement impairment we distinguish:
a) Children with mildly impaired movement: the child exhibits disorders in movement which cause a mild functional disorder, can walk autonomously also outside premises, but can experience difficulties in running or when walking for a longer period of time on an uneven terrain. They are independent in the execution of all tasks, with the exception of those which require good manual skills. They do not depend on aids and need only minor adaptations. For academic work they do not require any physical assistance but for certain tasks they might need some aids (special writing utensils, tools, table or chair).

b) Children with moderate movement impairments: the child exhibits disorders in movement that might cause a moderate functional impairment. Otherwise they can walk autonomously within premises or shorter distances. The use of aids might be required (special shoes, ortosis, crutches). They have difficulties walking on an uneven terrain and on stairs, where they tend to be slower and need supervision or the possibility to hold on to something or somebody. For medium or long distances they use a specially adapted bicycle or transport wheelchair, or a manually steered wheelchair. They might need the assistance or supervision of another person. The fine manual motor skills can be moderately impaired. In executing daily chores they need the supervision or support while for more demanding tasks they need adaptations or aids. The sphincter control can also be impaired, which is managed either by the child alone or with the help of supervision. In academic work they sometimes need the physical assistance of another person.

c) Children with severe movement impairments: the child exhibits disorders in movement which cause a severe functional disorder, otherwise they can walk autonomously short distances although walking short distances without aids is not functional. They can use ortosis and crutches part of the day. For the major part of moving within premises or outside they need a manually steered wheelchair. Outside they might also use an adapted bicycle or the assistance of another person. Walking on stairs is not possible. Fine motor skills are impaired and they obstruct good manual functions. For daily tasks they need constant partial assistance of another person. The possible disorders in sphincter control require pressing the bladder or self-catheterisation. For the majority of academic work they need physical assistance.

7. Children with long term illness Children with long term illness are children with long-lasting or chronic disorders and diseases which hinder them in their academic work. A chronic disease is any kind of disease which cannot be cured within three months. Chronic diseases are among other: cardiological, endocrinological, gastroenterological, allergological, rheumatological, nephrological, pulmological, oncological, haematological, dermatological diseases, psychiatric and neurological diseases (for example epilepsy), autoimmune and eating disorders.

8. Children with deficits in individual areas of learning (Pupils with severe specific learning disability)
Children with deficits in individual areas of learning are children where delays in development are observed due to known or unknown disorders in the functioning of the central nervous system. The disorders are connected with attention, memory, thinking, coordination, communication, the development of social skills and emotional maturation, whereby expressed difficulties can be observed in connection with reading, writing, spelling and arithmetic.

The deficits in specific learning areas can persist throughout a person's life and can affect one's learning and behaviour. The children can be identified as children with deficits in specific areas of learning only when the difficulties observed in the present schooling have not been possible to eliminate in spite of the adaptations in the methods and forms of work or by inclusion in additional lessons or other forms of individual and group support offered by the school as stipulated in the third paragraph of Article 12 and 14 of the Primary School Act, and when in spite of all the support in individual subject or subjects the child did not achieve the minimum knowledge standards. The disorders are primarily not connected with visual, hearing or motor disorders, disorders in mental development, emotional disorders or unsuitable environmental factors, which, however, can occur at the same time.

12. Children with boundary intelligence[11]
Besides the eight different groups of children with special needs (according to The Placement of Children with Special Needs Act) there are two additional ones: pupils with learning difficulties and gifted and talented (according to The Elementary School Act).

Cross-National Category B

9. Children with behavioural or emotional disorders
Children with behavioural or emotional disorders are those with dissocial behaviour which is intense, repeated, of permanent nature and is reflected in unsuccessful social integration. The child's dissocial behaviour can be externally or internally driven and is characterised by symptoms such as aggressive or

---

[11] As of March 2006 this category has not been used anymore

autoagressive behaviour, alcohol and drug abuse, destruction of foreign property, run away from home, emotional disorders.

The child can be identified as having behavioural and personality disorders only in cases when the treatment of the school counselling service and other professionals, social group and family has not led to the reduction of the described difficulties.

In spite of the fact that some of the behavioural states and patterns can be observed already in early childhood, the diagnosis for personality disorders should not be given until the child's personality development has been finished.

10. Pupils with learning difficulties

According to The Elementary School Act teachers have to adjust forms of teaching, organise supplement lessons and other forms of individual or group help for pupils with learning difficulties. Recently a national document was released ("Conception of work with pupils with learning difficulties in elementary school") about recognizing pupils with learning difficulties and providing possible means of help in school for them.

11. Gifted and talented (not applicable)

According to The Elementary School Act gifted and talented pupils are recognised as children with special needs. To provide suitable means of help for them we have a national document which regulates this field.

Annex 3. Starting and Ending Age of the Period of Compulsory Education

Figure A3. **Starting and ending age of the period of compulsory education**

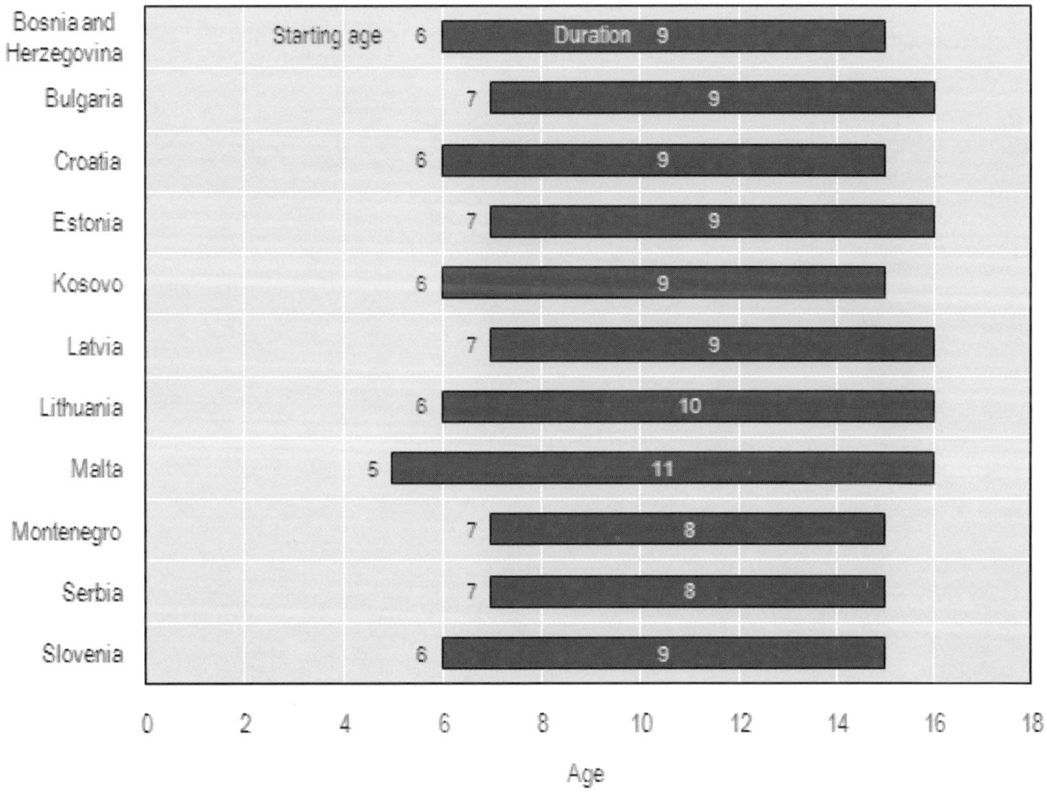

OECD PUBLISHING, 2, rue André-Pascal, 75775 PARIS CEDEX 16
PRINTED IN FRANCE
(91 2009 111 P) ISBN 978-92-64-07582-5 – No. 56985 2009